Poor Richard's Almanack of Common Sense:

An Original Compilation
Consisting of *Poor Richard's Almanack* and
Thomas Paine's *Common Sense*

By
Benjamin Franklin
Thomas Paine

Compiled
By
Joe Mitchell, MA

HISTORIC PUBLISHING
San Antonio, Texas

Poor Richard's Almanack

Benjamin Franklin

POOR RICHARD'S ALMANACK ∴ ∴ *by* BENJAMIN FRANKLIN

Selections from the apothegms and proverbs, with a brief sketch of the life of Benjamin Franklin.

Published by
THE U. S. C. PUBLISHING CO.
WATERLOO, IOWA

Opposite historic Old South Church in Boston, on January 6, 1706, was born Benjamin Franklin.

Benjamin was the fifteenth child of Josiah Franklin, whose occupation was that of tallow-chandler or candle-maker. Business was not prosperous, and the Franklin family was reared in very humble circumstances.

As a child, Benjamin hungered for books and knowledge. During the two years that his father was able to send him to school, he showed remarkable aptitude and industry, and rapidly outdistanced his fellow pupils.

The first book which Franklin read was Bunyan's "Pilgrim's Progress". By trading and borrowing, he managed to secure other volumes. His passion for reading was so intense that he attracted the attention of a kind-hearted Boston merchant, who gave the boy access to his well-stocked library. Franklin read only books which could add to his education, and read them with a thoroughness that extracted every bit of useful knowledge.

After leaving school, Franklin was apprenticed to his brother James in the printing trade. His wage was very small and he had to live most frugally.

James started a newspaper, and Benjamin set type and distributed the sheets. One day, he anonymously contributed some verses and apothegms and was overjoyed to find them accepted and published.

When his brother discovered that he was the contributor, an altercation broke out between the two, due principally to the ill temper of James. The quarrel was finally the cause of Benjamin's leaving Boston and going to Philadelphia.

In Philadelphia, Franklin obtained work with Keimer, a printer. His lodgings were found at the house of Mr. Read, with whose pretty daughter, Deborah, he promptly fell in love. Mrs. Read, however, counselled the two to postpone the marriage until Franklin should earn sufficient to maintain his own household. He was but eighteen years old at this time.

Sir William Keith, governor of the province of Pennsylvania, became acquainted with Franklin and offered to set him up in the printing business. Franklin, of course, accepted. At Keith's suggestion, he sailed to England to purchase an up-to-date outfit. Arrived there, he found that Keith was without credit. His beautiful plans went for naught and he was stranded in England without funds or prospects. It took him several years to work his way back to America.

When he returned, the first news to greet Franklin was the marriage of Deborah Read to another man.

At 22 years of age, Franklin had not made much progress toward the goal of his ambition. But nothing daunted, he applied himself with greater industry, greater self-sacrifice and greater perseverance. He kept plugging away at his trade of printer, and entered into business ventures with other men, all of which proved rapid failures. Finally, he struck out for himself. Coincidently, Deborah Read's husband died and Franklin took her to wife.

The young couple had to live on close margin for a few years. When Franklin was 27 years of age, he evolved the idea which opened the road to fame and fortune. This was Poor Richard's Almanack. The first number had a tremendous sale. His homely, trite, common-sense sayings achieved wide popularity and each succeeding issue found more subscribers than its predecessor. The general recognition and respect gained for Franklin through the Almanack gave him the opportunity to enter public life. This sphere of activity was greatly to his liking. He held important offices and introduced many splendid reforms into the municipal government.

Franklin's pet project was an efficient institution of learning. When he was 37 years old, his plans materialized into the founding of an academy from which has grown the great University of Pennsylvania.

The scientists of Europe were at this time becoming aware of a mysterious force which they named electricity. Musschenbroeck, a German, came forth with the discovery of the Leyden jar. Franklin immediately devoted himself to a study of electricity. The subject proved to interesting, so full of possibilities that he sold out his printing business in order to devote his entire effort to the new field. His business, started on nothing, brought the handsome price of $90,000.

When Franklin declared his belief that electricity and lightning were identical, the whole world laughed. He then made his famous kite test, and proved his theory. This demonstration gained world recognition for him as a scientist and won him many honors.

The colonies were now passing through the turbulent period preceding the Revolutionary War. Franklin was a foremost figure in public life, and became the commissioner of the colonies to England.

The first cause for provocation on the part of the colonies was the Stamp Act, which imposed an enormous tax on deeds, college degrees and printed matter. England sought to meet the expenses of the French-Indian war by this tax. Franklin's efficient representation and effective pleading secured its repeal in 1766.

However, one year later, Parliament enacted a more obnoxious bill, placing a heavy duty on tea, glass and other commodities. Then it was that certain indignant citizens of Boston held their Boston Tea Party and brought upon the heads of the community the ill-considered, hateful Boston Port Bill. The city was virtually put in a state of seizure by the British under General Gage.

This final action precipitated the crisis, and the Revolutionary War was on. Gage made his disastrous march to Concord and Lexington, and Bunker Hill ended in a triumph for American pluck.

Although in favor of settling the dispute by arbitration, Franklin was as zealous a patriot as any. He was a member of the first Continental Congress, and helped frame the Declaration of Independence. Later he went to Paris as special envoy to France for the colonies. He was received with great acclaimation and was accorded many honors. His mission of enlisting France's aid in the struggle was completely successful. Helped by the money of France and by the valor of such men as Lafayette, the Revolution triumphed.

After an absence from America of nine years, Franklin returned. He was given a royal reception. Although 77 years old now, he still gave his country the best that was in him, until his death on April 17, 1790. At his burial 20,000 persons gathered to do him respect and honor.

Franklin's life has been called the most interesting and the most successful lived by any American. And the explanation is found in the rule that guided him throughout his career: To go straight forward in doing what appears to be right, leaving the consequences to Providence.

Poor Richard's Almanack.

1. A child thinks 20 shillings and 20 years can scarce ever be spent.
2. A cold April, the barn will fill.
3. A countryman between two lawyers, is like a fish between two cats.
4.* Act uprightly, and despise calumny; dirt may stick to a mud wall, but not to polish'd marble.
5. A cypher and humility make the other figures and virtues of tenfold value.
6. A false friend and a shadow attend only while the sun shines.
7.* A father's a treasure; a brother's a comfort; a friend is both.
8. A fat kitchen, a lean will.
9. A fine genius in his own country, is like gold in the mine.
10. A flatterer never seems absurd: The flatter'd always takes his word.
11.* After three days men grow weary of a wench, a guest, and weather rainy.
12. After crosses and losses men grow humbler and wiser.

13. A full belly is the mother of all evil.
14. A full belly makes a dull brain.
15. A good example is the best sermon.
16. A good lawyer, a bad neighbor.
17. A good man is seldom uneasy, an ill one never easy.
18. A house without woman and firelight, is like a body without soul or sprite.
19. A lean award is better than a fat judgment.
20. A learned blockhead is a greater blockhead than an ignorant one.
21.* A lie stands on one leg, truth on two.
22. A life of leisure, and a life of laziness, are two things.
23. A light purse is a heavy curse.
24. A little house well fill'd, a little field well till'd, and a little wife well will'd, are great riches.
25. All blood is alike ancient.
26. All mankind are beholden to him that is kind to the good.
27.* All things are cheap to the saving, dear to the wasteful.
28.* All things are easy to industry, all things difficult to sloth.

29. All would live long, but none would be old.

30. A long life may not be good enough, but a good life is long enough.

31. A man in a passion rides a mad horse.

32. A man without a wife, is but a half a man.

33. A man without ceremony has need of great merit in its place.

34. Ambition often spends foolishly what avarice had wickedly collected.

35. A mob's a monster; heads enough, but no brains.

36. A modern wit is one of David's fools.

37. An egg today is better than a hen to-morrow.

38. An empty bag cannot stand upright.

39.* A new truth is a truth, an old error is an error, though Clodpate won't allow either.

40. Anger and folly walk cheek by jole; repentance treads on both their heels.

41. Anger is never without a reason, but seldom with a good one.

42. Anger warms the invention, but overheats the oven.

43. An honest man will receive neither money nor praise, that is not his due.

44. An hundred thieves cannot strip one naked man, especially if his skin's off.

45. An ill wound, but not an ill name, may be healed.

46. An innocent plowman is more worthy than a vicious prince.

47.* Anoint a villian and he'll stab you; stab him, and he'll anoint you.

48. An old man in a house is a good sign.

49. An old young man will be a young old man.

50. An ounce of wit that is bought, is worth a pound that is taught.

51. An undutiful daughter, will prove an unmanageable wife.

52. A pair of good ears will drain dry an hundred tongues.

53. A plowman on his legs is higher than a gentleman on his knees.

54. Approve not of him that commends all you say.

55. A quarrelsome man has no good neighbors.

56. A quiet conscience sleeps in thunder.

57.* Are you angry that others disappoint you? Remember you cannot depend upon yourself.

58. As charms are nonsense, nonsense is a charm.

59. Ask and have, is sometimes dear buying.

60. A soft tongue may strike hard.

61. As pride increases, fortune declines.

62.* As sore places meet most rubs, proud folks meet most affronts.

63. A temper to bear much, will have much to bear.

64. A wicked hero will turn his back to an innocent coward.

65. As we must account for every idle word, so we must for every idle silence.

66. At a great pennyworth, pause a while.

67. A traveller should have a hog's nose, deer's legs, and an ass's back.

68. At the working man's house hunger looks in but dares not enter.

69.* At 20 years of age the will reigns; at thirty the wit; at 40 the judgment.

70. Bad commentators spoil the best of books.

71. Bad gains are truly losses.

72. Bargaining has neither friends nor relations.

73. Be always ashamed to catch thyself idle.

74.* Be at war with your vices, at peace with your neighbors.

75. Beauty and folly are old companions.

76. Being ignorant is not so much a shame, as being unwilling to learn.

77. Ben beats his pate, and fancys wit will come; but he may knock, there's nobody at home.

78. Be not niggardly of what costs thee nothing, as courtesy, counsel, and countenance.

79. Be slow in choosing a friend, slower in changing.

80. Better is a little with content than much with contention.

81. Better slip with foot than tongue.

82. Beware, beware! He'll cheat without scruple, who can without fear.

83. Beware of him that is slow to anger; he is angry for something, and will not be pleased for nothing.

84.* Beware of little expenses, a small leak will sink a great ship.

85.* Beware of meat twice boil'd, and an old foe reconcil'd.

86.* Beware of the young doctor and the old barber.

87. Blame-all and praise-all are two block heads.

88. Blessed is he that expects nothing, for he shall never be disappointed.

89. Buy what thou hast no need of; and e'er long thou shalt sell thy necessaries.

90. By diligence and patience, the mouse bit in two the cable.

91. Calamity and prosperity are the touchstones of integrity.

92. Ceremony is not civility; nor civility ceremony.

93.* Changing countries or beds, cures neither a bad manager, nor a fever.

94. Cheese and salt meat should be sparingly eat.

95.* Children and princes will quarrel for trifles.

96. Clean your finger, before you point at my spots.

97. Clearly spoken, Mr. Fog! You explain English by Greek.

98.* Content and riches seldom meet together. Riches take thou, contentment I had rather.

99. Content is the philosopher's stone, that turns all it touches into gold.

100.* Content makes poor men rich; discontent makes rich men poor.

101. Courage would fight, but discretion won't let him.

102. Creditors have better memories than debtors.

103.* Cut the wings of your hens and hopes, lest they lead you a wary dance after them.

104. Danger is sauce for prayers.

105.* Dally not with other folks' women or money.

106. Death takes no bribes.

107. Declaiming against pride, is not always a sign of humility.

108.* Defer not thy well doing; be not like St. George, who is always on horseback, and never rides on.

109. Deny self for self's sake.

110.* Despair ruins some, presumption many.

111.* Different sects like different clocks, may be all near the matter, though they don't quite agree.

112. Diligence is the mother of good luck.

113.* Diligence overcomes difficulties, sloth makes them.

114. Distrust and caution are the parents of security.

115.* Do good to thy friend to keep him, to thy enemy to gain him.

116.* Doing an injury puts you below your enemy; revenging one makes you but even with him; forgiving, it sets you above him.

117. Do not do that which you would not have known.

118. Do me the favor to deny me at once.

119.* Don't go to the doctor with every distemper, nor to the lawyer with every quarrel, nor to the pot for every thirst.

120.* Don't judge of men's wealth or piety, by their Sunday appearances.

121.* Don't misinform your doctor nor your lawyer.

122. Don't overload gratitude; if you do she'll kick.

123. Don't think to hunt two hares with one dog.

124. Don't throw stones at your neighbors, if your own windows are glass.

125. Don't value a man for the quality he is of, but for the qualities he possesses.

126. Dost thou love life? Then do not squander time; for that's the stuff life is made of.

127. Drink does not drown care, but waters it, and makes it grow faster.

128.* Drink water; put the money in your pocket, and leave the dry-bellyache in the punch-bowl.

129. Drive thy business, or it will drive thee.

130.* Drunkenness, that worst of evils, makes some men fools, some beasts, some devils.

131. Early to bed and early to rise, makes a man healthy, wealthy, and wise.

132. Eat few suppers, and you'll need few medicines.

133.* Eat to please thyself, but dress to please others.

134. Employ thy time well, if thou meanest to gain leisure.

135. Ever since follies have pleased, fools have been able to divert.

136.* Every man has assurance enough to boast of his honesty, few of their understanding.

137. Experience keeps a dear school, yet fools will learn in no other.

138. Eyes and priests bear no jests.

139. Fear God, and your enemies will fear you.

140.* Fear not death; for the sooner we die, the longer shall we be immortal.

141. Fear to do ill, and you need fear nought else.

142.* Fine linen, girls and gold so bright, choose not to take by candle light.

143.* Fish and visitors stink in three days.

144. Fly pleasures and they'll follow you.

145.* Fond pride of dress is sure an empty curse; e'er fancy you consult, consult your purse.

146. Fools make feasts, and wise men eat 'em.

147. Fools multiply folly.

148.* Fools need advice most, but wise men only are the better for it.

149.* For age and want save while you may; no morning sun lasts a whole day.

150. For one poor man there are an hundred indigent.

151.* For want of a nail the shoe is lost; for want of a shoe, the horse is lost; for want of a horse the rider is lost.

152. Friendship cannot live with ceremony, nor without civility.

153. Friendship increases by visiting friends, but by visiting seldom.

154. Full of courtesy, full of craft.

155. Generous minds are all of kin.

156. Genius without education is like silver in the mine.

157. Gifts burst rocks.

158. Gifts much expected, are paid, not given.

159.* Give me yesterday's bread, this day's flesh, and last year's cyder.

160.* Glass, china, and reputation are easily crack'd, and never well mended.

161. God gives all things to industry.

162. God heals, and the doctor takes the fees.

163. God helps them that help themselves.

164. God, parents, and instructors, can never be requited.

165. Good sense is a thing all need, few have, and none think they want.

166. Good wives and good plantations are made by good husbands.

167. Grace thou thy house, and let not that grace thee.

168. Graft good fruit all, or graft not at all.

169. Great almsgiving, lessens no man's living.

170.* Great estates may venture more; little boats must keep near shore.

171. Great famine when wolves eat wolves.

172. Great good-nature, without prudence, is a great misfortune.

173.* Great merit is coy, as well as great pride.

174. Great modesty often hides great merit.

175. Great spenders are bad lenders.

176. Great talkers, little doers.

177. Great talkers should be cropt, for they've no need of ears.

178. Half hospitality opens his door and shuts up his countenance.

179. Half the truth is often a great lie.

180. Half wits talk much but say little.

181. Happy that Nation, fortunate that age, whose history is not diverting.

182. Happy's the wooing that's not long a doing.

183. Happy Tom Crump, ne'er sees his own hump.

184. Haste makes waste.

185. Harry Smatter, has a mouth for every matter.

186. Have you somewhat to do to-morrow; do it to-day.

187. Having been poor is no shame, but being ashamed of it, is.

188. Hear no ill of a friend, nor speak any of an enemy.

189. Hear reason, or she'll make you feel her.

190. He does not possess wealth, it possesses him.

191. He has chang'd his one ey'd horse for a blind one.

192. He has lost his boots, but sav'd his spurs.

193.* He is a governor that governs his passions, and he a servant that serves them.

194. He is ill clothed, who is bare of virtue.

195. He is no clown that drives the plow, but he that doth clownish things.

196. He is not well bred, that cannot bear ill-breeding in others.

197. Help, hands; for I have no lands.

198. He makes a foe, who makes a jest.

199. Here comes the orator, with his flood of words, and his drop of reason.

200. He's a fool that cannot conceal his wisdom.

201. He's a fool that makes his doctor his heir.

202. He's gone, and forgot nothing but to say farewell—to his creditors.

203. He's the best physician that knows the worthlessness of the most medicines.

204. He that best understands the world, least likes it.

205.* He that builds before he counts the cost, acts foolishly; and he that counts before he builds, finds he did not count wisely.

206. He that buys by the penny, maintains not only himself, but other people.

207. He that by the plow would thrive, himself must either hold or drive.

208. He that can bear a reproof, and mend by it, if he is not wise, is in a fair way of being so.

209. He that can compose himself, is wiser than he that composes books.

210. He that can have patience can have what he will.

211. He that cannot bear with other people's passions, cannot govern his own.

212. He that cannot obey, cannot command.

213. He that can take rest is greater than he that can take cities.

214. He that can travel well afoot, keeps a good horse.

215. He that doth what he should not, shall feel what he would not.

216. He that drinks fast, pays slow.

217. He that drinks his cyder alone, let him catch his horse alone.

218. He that falls in love with himself, will have no rivals.

219. He that goes far to marry, will either deceive or be deceived.

220. He that has a trade, has an office of profit and honor.

221. He that has not got a wife, is not yet a complete man.

222. He that hath a trade, hath an estate.

223. He that is of opinion money will do everything may well be suspected of doing everything for money.

224.* He that is rich need not live sparingly, and he that can live sparingly, need not be rich.

225. He that lies down with dogs, shall rise up with fleas.

226. He that never eats too much, will never be lazy.

227. He that pays for work before it's done, has but a penny-worth for two pence.

228. He that pursues two hares at once, does not catch one and let t'other go.

229. He that resolves to mend hereafter, resolves not to mend now.

230. He that riseth late, must trot all day, and shall scarce overtake his business by night.

231. He that scatters thorns, let him not go barefoot.

232.* He that's content hath enough; he that complains has too much.

233. He that sells upon trust, loses many friends, and always wants money.

234. He that sows thorns, should never go barefoot.

235. He that speaks ill of the mare, will buy her.

236. He that speaks much, is much mistaken.

237.* He that spills the rum loses that only; he that drinks it, often loses both that and himself.

238. He that takes a wife, takes care.

239. He that waits upon fortune, is never sure of a dinner.

240. He that won't be counsell'd, can't be help'd.

241. He that would catch fish, must venture his bait.

242. He that would have a short Lent, let him borrow money to be repaid at Easter.

243. He that would live in peace and at ease, must not speak all he knows, nor judge all he sees.

244. He that would rise at court, must begin by creeping.

245. He that would travel much, should eat little.

246. He who multiplies riches multiplies cares.

247.* He who buys had need have 100 eyes, but one's enough for him that sells the stuff.

248.* Hold your council before dinner; the full belly hates thinking as well as acting.

249. Honors change manners.

250. Honor thy father and mother, i. e., live so as to be an honor to them when they are dead.

251.* Hope and a red rag, are baits for men and mackrel.

252. Hope of gain lessens pain.

253. How few there are who have courage enough to own their faults.

254. Hunger is the best pickle.

255. Hunger never saw bad bread.

256. Idleness is the Dead Sea, that swallows all virtues.

257. Idleness is the greatest prodigality.

258. If it were not for the belly, the back might wear gold.

259. If Jack's in love, he's no judge of Jill's beauty.

260. If man could have half his wishes, he would double his troubles.

261. If passion drives, let reason hold the reins.

262. If pride leads the van, beggary brings up the rear.

263. If thou hast wit and learning, add to it wisdom and modesty.

264. If thou injurest conscience, it will have its revenge on thee.

265.* If thou would'st live long, live well; for folly and wickedness shorten life.

266. If wind blows on you thro' a hole, make your will and take care of your soul.

267. If worldly goods cannot save me from death, they ought not to hinder me to eternal life.

268. If you'd be belov'd, make yourself amiable.

269. If you desire many things, many things seem but a few.

270. If you'd have a servant that you like, serve yourself.

271.* If you'd have it done, go; if not, send.

272. If you'd know the value of money, go and borrow some.

273. If you'd lose a troublesome visitor, lend him money.

274. If you do what you would not, you must hear what you would not.

275. If you have no money in your pot, have some in your mouth.

276. If you have time don't wait for time.

277. If you know how to spend less than you get, you have the philisopher's stone.

278. If your head is wax, don't walk in the sun.

279.* If you ride a horse, sit close and tight, if you ride a man, sit easy and light.

280. If your riches are yours, why don't you take them with you to the other world?

281. If you would be loved, love and be lovable.

282. If you would be reveng'd of your enemy, govern yourself.

283. If you would have guests merry with cheer, be so yourself, or so at least appear.

284. If you would keep your secret from an enemy, tell it not to a friend.

285. If you would not be forgotten as soon as you are dead and rotten, either write things worth reading, or do things worth writing.

286. If you would reap praise you must sow the seeds, gentle words and useful deeds.

287.* Ignorance leads men into a party, and shame keeps them from getting out again.

288.* I have never seen the philosopher's stone that turns lead into gold, but I have known the pursuit of it turn a man's gold into lead.

289.* Ill company is like a dog who dirts those most, that he loves best.

290. Ill customs and bad advice are seldom forgotten.

291.* "I'll warrant ye", goes before rashness; "Who'd-a-tho't" comes sneaking after.

292.* Industry pays debts, despair increases them.

293. In success be moderate.

294. Interest which blinds some people, enlightens others.

295. In the affairs of this world men are saved, not by faith, but by the want of it.

296. I saw few die of hunger, of eating 100,000.

297. Is there anything men take more pains about than to render themselves unhappy?

298. It is better to take many injuries, than to give one.

299.* It is ill jesting with the joiner's tools, worse with the doctor's.

300.* It is ill-manners to silence a fool, and cruelty to let him go on.

301. It is not leisure that is not used.

302.* It is wise not to seek a secret, and honest not to reveal it.

303. It's common for men to give pretended reasons instead of one real one.

304. It's the easiest thing in the world for a man to deceive himself.

305. Jack Little sow'd little, and little he'll reap.

306.* Keep flax from fire, youth from gaming.

307.* Keep thou from the opportunity, and God will keep thee from the sin.

308. Keep thy shop, and thy shop will keep thee.

309.* Keep your eyes wide open before marriage, half shut afterwards.

310. Keep your mouth wet, feet dry.

311.* Kings and bears often worry their keepers.

312.* Kings have long arms, but misfortune longer; let none think themselves out of her reach.

313. Late children, early orphans.

314.* Laws like to cobwebs, catch small flies, great ones break through before your eyes.

315.* Laws too gentle are seldom obeyed; too severe, seldom executed.

316. Laziness travels so slowly, that poverty soon overtakes him.

317.* Learn of the skillful; he that teaches himself, hath a fool for his master.

318. Lend money to an enemy, and thou'lt gain him, to a friend and thou'lt lose him.

319.* Let all men know thee, but no man know thee thoroughly; men freely ford that see the shallows.

320. Let every new year find you a better man.

321. Let thy child's first lesson be obedience, and the second may be what thou wilt.

322.* Let thy discontents be thy secrets; —if the world knows them 'twill despise thee and increase them.

323. Let thy maid-servant be faithful, strong, and homely.

324. Let thy vices die before thee.

325. Liberality is not giving much, but giving wisely.

326. Light gains, heavy purses.

327. Light heel'd mothers make leaden-heel'd daughters.

328. Light purse, heavy heart.

329. Little rogues easily become great ones.

330. Little strokes fell great oaks.

331. Look before, or you'll find yourself behind.

332. Lost time is never found again.

333. Love, and be loved.

334.* Love, cough, and a smoke, can't well be hid.

335.* Lover and Lordship hate companions.

336.* Lovers, travellers, and poets will give money to be heard.

337. Love well, whip well.

338. Love your enemies, for they tell you your faults.

339. Love your neighbor; yet don't pull down your hedge.

340. Lying rides upon debt's back.

341.* Mad kings and mad bulls, are not to be held by treaties and packthread.

342. Many a man's own tongue gives evidence against his understanding.

343. Many a man would have been worse, if his estate had been better.

344. Many a meal is lost for want of meat.

345. Many complain of their memory, few of their judgment.

346. Many dishes, many diseases.

347. Many estates are spent in the getting.

348. Many foxes grow grey, but few grow good.

349. Many have quarrel'd about religion, that never practic'd it.

350. Many medicines, few cures.

351. Many princes sin with David, but few repent with him.

352. Many would live by their wits, but break for want of stock.

353. Marry above thy match, and thou'lt get a master.

354.* Marry your son when you will, but your daughter when you can.

355. Mary's mouth costs her nothing, for she never opens it but at others expense.

356. Meanness is the parent of insolence.

357.* Men and melons are hard to know.

358.* Men differ daily about things which are subject to sense, is it likely then they should agree about things invisible?

359.* Men meet, mountains never.

360. Men often mistake themselves, seldom forget themselves.

361. Men take more pains to mask than mend.

362. Money and good manners make the gentleman.

363.* Money and man a mutual friendship show; man makes false money, money makes man so.

364. Most fools think they are only ignorant.

365. Most of the learning in use, is of no great use.

366.* Most people return small favors, acknowledge middling ones, and repay great ones with ingratitude.

367.* Much virtue in herbs, little in men.

368. Necessity has no law; I know some attorneys of the same.

369. Necessity has no law; Why? Because, 'tis not to be had without money.

370. Necessity never made a good bargain.

371. Ne'er take a wife till thou hast a house (and a fire) to put her in.

372.* Neglect kills injuries, revenge increases them.

373. Neglect mending a small fault, and 'twill soon be a great one.

374. Neither praise nor dispraise, till seven Christmasses be over.

375. Never intreat a servant to dwell with thee.

376.* Never praise your cyder, horse, or bedfellow.

377. Never spare the parson's wine, nor the baker's pudding.

378. Nice eaters seldom meet with a good dinner.

379. Nick's passions grow fat and hearty; his understanding looks consumptive.

380. Nine men in ten are suicides.

381. No gains without pains.

382. No man e'er was glorious who was not laborious.

383. None are deceived but they that confide.

384.* None know the unfortunate, and the fortunate do not know themselves.

385. None preaches better than the ant, and she says nothing.

386. No resolution repenting hereafter, can be sincere.

387.* Nor eye in a letter, nor hand in a purse, nor ear in the secret of another.

388. Nothing but money is sweeter than honey.

389. Nothing drys sooner than a tear.

390. Nothing humbler than ambition, when it is about to climb.

391. Nothing more like a fool, than a drunken man.

392. Nothing so popular as goodness.

393. Now I've a sheep and a cow, every body bids me good morrow.

394. No wood without bark.

395.* No workman without tools, nor lawyer without fools, can live by their rules.

396. Observe all men; thyself most.

397. Observe old Vellum; he praises former times, as if he'd a mind to sell 'em.

398. Of learned fools I have seen ten times ten; of unlearned wise men I have seen a hundred.

399. O Lazy-bones! Dost thou think God would have given thee arms and legs, if he had not design'd thou should'st use them.

400. Old boys have their playthings as well as young ones; the difference is only in the price.

401. Old young and old long.

402.* One good husband is worth two good wives; for the scarcer things are the more they're valued.

403. One may be more cunning than another, but not more cunning than everybody else.

404.* One mend-fault is worth two find-faults, but one find-fault is better than two make-faults.

405. One to-day is worth two to-morrows.

406.* Onions can make ev'n heirs and widows weep.

407.* Pain wastes the body; pleasures the understanding.

408. Pardoning the bad, is injuring the good.

409. Patience in market, is worth pounds in a year.

410. Pay what you owe, and you'll know what's your own.

411. Philosophy as well as foppery often changes fashion.

412. Plough deep, while sluggards sleep.

413. Pollio, who values nothing that's within, buys books as men hunt beavers,—for their skin.

414. Poor Dick eats like a well man, and drinks like a sick.

415. Poor Plain Dealing! Dead without issue.

416.* Poverty, poetry, and new titles of honor, make men ridiculous.

417.* Poverty wants some things, luxury many things, avarice all things.

418. Praise to the undeserving is severe satire.

419. Pray, don't burn my house to roast your eggs.

420. Prayers and provender hinder no journey.

421. Presumption first blinds a man, then sets him a running.

422. Pretty and witty, will wound if they hit ye.

423.* Pride and the gout are seldom cur'd throughout.

424. Pride breakfasted with plenty, dined with poverty, supped with infamy.

425. Pride dines upon vanity, sups on contempt.

426. Pride is as loud a beggar as want, and a great deal more saucy.

427. Pride gets into the coach, and shame mounts behind.

428. Proclaim not all thou knowest, all thou owest, all thou hast, nor all thou canst.

429. Prodigality of time, produces poverty of mind as well as of estate.

430. Promises may get thee friends, but non-performance will turn them into enemies.

431.* Proud modern learning despises the ancient. School-men are now laughed at by school-boys.

432. Quarrels never could last long, if on one side only lay the wrong.

433. Rather go to bed supperless, than run in debt for a breakfast.

434.* Reading makes a full man, meditation a profound man, discourse a clear man.

435. Read much, but not many books.

436.* Retirement does not always secure virtue; Lot was upright in the city, wicked in the mountain.

437. Rob not for burnt offerings.

438.* Rob not God, nor the poor, lest thou ruin thyself; the eagle snatched a coal from the altar, but it fired her nest.

439. Samson with his strong body, had a weak head, or he would not have laid in a harlot's lap.

440. Saying and doing have quarrel'd and parted.

441.* Search others for their virtues, thyself for thy vices.

442.* Sell not virtue to purchase wealth, nor liberty to purchase power.

443.* Silence is not always a sign of wisdom, but babbling is ever a mark of folly.

444. Silks and satins put out the kitchen fire.

445. Since thou art not sure of a minute, throw not away an hour.

446.* Singularity in the right, hath ruined many; happy those who are convinced of the general opinion.

447. Sleep without supping, and you'll rise without owing for it.

448. Sloth and silence are a fool's virtues.

449.* Sloth (like rust) consumes faster than labor wears. The used key is always bright.

450. Snowy winter, a plentiful harvest.

451.* Some are justly laughed at for keeping their money foolishly, others for spending it idly; he is the greatest fool that lays it out in a purchase of repentance.

452. Some are weatherwise, some are otherwise.

453. Some make conscience of wearing a hat in the church, who make none of robbing the altar.

454. Sorrow is good for nothing but sin.

455. Spare and have is better than spend and crave.

456.* Speak and speed; the close mouth catches no flies.

457. Speak little, do much.

458.* Speak with contempt of none, from slave to king; the meanest bee hath, and will use, a sting.

459. Strange! that a man who has wit enough to write a satire, should have folly enough to publish it.

460. Strange, that he who lives by shifts, can seldom shift himself.

461.* Strive to be the greatest man in your country, and you may be disappointed; strive to be the best, and you may succeed; he may well win the race that runs by himself.

462. Success has ruin'd many a man.

463.* Sudden power is apt to be insolent, sudden liberty saucy; that behaves best which has grown gradually.

464. Suspicion may be no fault, but showing it may be a great one.

465.* Take counsel in wine, but resolve afterwards in water.

466. Take courage, mortal; death can't banish thee out of the universe.

467. Take heed of the vinegar of sweet wine, and the anger of good-nature.

468. Take this remark from Richard, poor and lame, whate'er is begun in anger, ends in shame.

469.* Talking against religion is unchaining a tiger; the beast let loose may worry his deliverer.

470.* Tart words make no friends; a spoonful of honey will catch more flies than a gallon of vinegar.

471. Teach your child to hold his tongue, he'll learn fast enough to speak.

472.* Tell a miser he's rich, and a woman she's old, you'll get no money of one, nor kindness of t'other.

473. Tell me my faults, and mend your own.

474. The absent are never without fault, nor the present without excuse.

475.* The ancients tell us what is best, but we must learn of the moderns what is fittest.

476. The bell calls others to church, but itself never minds the sermon.

477. The bird that sits, is easily shot.

478. The brave and the wise can both pity and excuse, when cowards and fools shew no mercy.

479.* The busy man has few idle visitors; to the boiling pot the flies come not.

480. The cat in gloves catches no mice.

481. The creditors are a superstitious sect, great observers of set days and times.

482.* The cunning man steals a horse, the wise man lets him alone.

493. The devil sweetens poison with honey.

484. The discontented man finds no easy chair.

485. The doors of wisdom are never shut.

486. The end of passion is the beginning of repentance.

487.* The excellency of hogs is fatness, of men virtue.

488. The eye of a master, will do more work than his hand.

489. The family of fools is ancient.

490. The favor of the great is no inheritance.

491. The generous mind least regards money, and yet most feels the want of it.

492. The golden age never was the present age.

493. The good pay-master is lord of another man's purse.

494. The good or ill hap of a good or ill life, is the good or ill choice of a good or ill wife.

495.* The heart of the fool is in his mouth, but the mouth of the wise man is in his heart.

496. The heathens when they dy'd, went to bed without a candle.

497.* The honest man takes pains, and then enjoys pleasures; the knave takes pleasures, and then suffers pains.

498.* The honey is sweet, but the bee has a sting.

499. The horse thinks one thing, and he that saddles him another.

500. The idle man is the devil's hireling; whose livery is rags, whose diet and wages are famine and diseases.

501. The king's cheese is half wasted in parings; but no matter, 'tis made of the people's milk.

502. The learned fool writes his nonsense in better language than the unlearned; but still 'tis nonsense.

503.* The magistrate should obey the laws, the people should obey the magistrate.

504. The master's eye wil do more work than both his hands.

505. The miser's cheese is wholesom'st.

506. The most exquisite folly is made of wisdom spun too fine.

507. The muses love the morning.

508. The nearest way to come to glory, is to do that for conscience which we do for glory.

509. The noblest question in the world is, what good may I do in it?

510.* The old man has given all to his son; O fool! to undress thyself before thou art going to bed.

511.* The painful preacher, like a candle bright, consumes himself in giving others light.

512. The poor have little, beggars none, the rich too much, enough not one.

513.* The poor man must walk to get meat for his stomach, the rich man to get a stomach to his meat.

514. The prodigal generally does more injustice than the covetous.

515.* The proof of gold is fire; the proof of woman, gold; the proof of man, a woman.

516. The proud hate pride—in others.

517. There are lazy minds as well as lazy bodies.

518. There are no fools so troublesome as those that have wit.

519.* There are no ugly loves, nor handsome prisons.

520. There are three faithful friends, an old wife, an old dog, and ready money.

521.* There are three things extremely hard, steel, a diamond and to know one's self.

522. There is neither honor nor gain got in dealing with a villian.

523. There is no little enemy.

524. There is no man so bad but he secretly respects the good.

525. There is much difference between imitating a good man, and counterfeiting him.

526. There's a time to wink as well as to see.

527. There're many witty men whose brains can't fill their bellies.

528. There's more old drunkards, than old doctors.

529. There's none deceived but he that trusts.

530. There's small revenge in words, but words may be greatly revenged.

531. There was never a good knife made of bad steel.

532. They who have nothing to trouble them, will be troubled at nothing.

533.* The rivers and bad governments, the lightest things swim at top.

534. The rotten apple spoils his companion.

535. The royal crown cures not the headache.

536. The same man cannot be both friend and flatterer.

537. The sleeping fox catches no poultry. Up! up!

538. The second vice is lying; the first is running in debt.

539. The sting of a reproach is the truth of it.

540. The sun never repents of the good he does, nor does he ever demand a recompence.

541. The things which hurt, instruct.

542. The tongue is ever turning to the aching tooth.

543. The tongue offends, and the ears get the cuffing.

544. The too obliging temper is evermore disobliging itself.

545. The way to be safe, is never to be secure.

546.* The way to see by faith, is to shut the Eye of Reason. The morning daylight appears plainer when you put out your candle.

547. The wise man draws more advantage from his enemies, than the fool from his friends.

548. The worst wheel of the cart makes the most noise.

549.* The wolf sheds his coat once a year, his disposition never.

550.* Think of three things, whence you came, where you are going, and to whom you must account.

551. Thirst after desert, not reward.

552.* Tho' modesty is a virtue, bashfulness is a vice.

553. Those that have much business must have much pardon.

554. Those who are fear'd, are hated.

555. Those who in quarrels interpose, must often wipe a bloody nose.

556. Tho' the mastiff be gentle, yet bite him not by the lip.

557. Thou canst not joke an enemy into a friend; but thou may'st a friend into an enemy.

558. Three good meals a day is bad living.

559. Three may keep a secret, if two of them are dead.

560.* Three things are men most likely to be cheated in, a horse, a wig, and a wife.

561.* Tim and his handsaw are good in their place, tho' not fit for preaching or shaving a face.

562. Time enough always proves little enough.

563. Time is an herb that cures all diseases.

564.* Tim was so learned, that he could name a horse in nine languages. So ignorant, that he bought a cow to ride on.

565.* 'Tis against some men's principle to pay interest, and seems against others' interest to pay the principal.

566. 'Tis a laudable ambition, that aims at being better than his neighbors.

567. 'Tis a shame that your family is an honor to you! You ought to be an honor to your family.

568.* 'Tis a strange forest that has no rotten wood in it, and a strange kindred that all are good in it.

569. 'Tis better leave for an enemy at one's death, than beg of a friend in one's life.

570. 'Tis easier to build two chimneys, than maintain one in fuel.

571. 'Tis easier to prevent bad habits than to break them.

572. 'Tis easy to see, hard to foresee.

573. 'Tis easier to suppress the first desire, than to satisfy all that follow it.

574. 'Tis great confidence in a friend to tell him your faults, greater to tell him his.

575. 'Tis hard (but glorious) to be poor and honest.

576.* 'Tis less discredit to abridge petty charges, than to stoop to petty gettings.

577. 'Tis not a holiday that's not kept holy.

578. 'Tis a well spent penny that saves a groat.

579. To bear other people's afflictions, every one has courage enough, and to spare.

580.* To be intimate with a foolish friend, is like going to bed with a razor.

581.* To be proud of knowledge, is to be blind with light; to be proud of virtue, is to poison yourself with the antidote.

582. To-day is yesterday's pupil.

583.* To err is human, to repent divine, to persist devilish.

584. To lengthen thy life, lessen thy meals.

585. To-morrow every fault is to be amended; but that to-morrow never comes.

586.* Tom, vain's your pains; they all will fail; ne'er was good arrow made of a sow's tail.

587. Tongue double, brings trouble.

588. Too much plenty makes mouth dainty.

589. To whom thy secret thou dost tell, to him thy freedom thou dost sell.

590. Tricks and treachery are the practice of fools, that have not wit enough to be honest.

591.* Trouble springs from idleness; toil from ease.

592. Trust thyself, and another shall not betray thee.

593. Two dry sticks will burn a green one.

594.* Up, sluggard, and waste not life; in the grave will be sleeping enough.

595. Vain-glory flowereth, but beareth no fruit.

596. Vanity backbites more than malice.

597. Vice knows she's ugly, so puts on her mask.

598. Virtue and a trade, are a child's best portion.

599. Virtue and happiness are mother and daughter.

600.* Virtue may not always make a face handsome, but vice will certainly make it ugly.

601.* Visits should be short, like a winter's day; lest you're too troublesome hasten away.

602.* Visit your aunt, but not every day; and call at your brother's, but not every night.

603. Want of care does us more damage than want of knowledge.

604. Wars bring scars.

605.* We are not so sensible of the greatest health as of the least sickness.

606. Wealth is not his that has it, but his that enjoys it.

607. Weighty questions ask for deliberate answers.

608. Welcome, mischief, if thou comest alone.

609. Well done is better than well said.

610. Well done, is twice done.

611. We may give advice, but we cannot give conduct.

612.* What is a butterfly at best? He's but a caterpillar dressed, the gaudy fop's his picture just.

613.* What's given shines, what's receiv'd is rusty.

614. What signifies knowing the names, if you know not the nature of things.

615. What signifies your patience, if you can't find it when you want it.

616.* What's proper is becoming; see the blacksmith with his white silk apron.

617. What you would seem to be, be really.

618. When a friend deals with a friend, let the bargain be clear and well penn'd, that they may continue friends to the end.

619.* When befriended, remember it; when you befriend, forget it.

620.* When death puts out your flame, the snuff will tell, if we were wax or tallow by the smell.

621. When knaves betray each other, one can scarce be blamed or the other pitied.

622.* When knaves fall out, honest men get their goods; when priests dispute, we come at the truth.

623. When out of favor, none know thee; when in, thou dost not know thyself.

624. When prosperity was well mounted, she let go the bridle, and soon came tumbling out of the saddle.

625. When reason preaches, if you won't hear her, she'll box your ears.

626. When there's more malice shown than matter, on the writer falls the satire.

627. When the well's dry, we know the worth of water.

628. When the wine enters, out goes the truth.

629. When 'tis fair, be sure take your coat with you.

630. When you're good to others, you are best to yourself.

631.* When you speak to a man, look on his eyes; when he speaks to thee, look on his mouth.

632. When you taste honey, remember gall.

633. Where bread is wanting, all's to be sold.

634. Where good laws are, much people flock thither.

635. Where sense is wanting, everything is wanting.

636. Where there's no law, there's no bread.

637.* Where there is hunger, law is not regarded; and where law is not regarded, there will be hunger.

638. Where there's marriage without love, there will be love without marriage.

639. Where yet was ever found the mother, who'd change her baby for another?

640.* Wide will wear, but narrow will tear.

641.* Wink at small faults; remember thou hast great ones.

642. Wish not so much to live long as to live well.

643. Without justice courage is weak.

644. With the old almanack and the old year, leave thy old vice, tho' ever so dear.

645. Who dainties love, shall beggars prove.

646. Who has deceiv'd thee so oft as thyself?

647. Who is powerful? He that governs his passions.

648. Who is rich? He that is content.

649. Who is rich? He that rejoices in his portion.

650. Who is strong? He that can conquer his bad habits.

651. Who is wise? He that learns from every one.

652. Who judges best of a man, his enemies or himself?

653. Who knows a fool, must know his brother; for one will recommend another.

654. Willows are weak, but they bind the faggot.

655. Wish a miser long life, and you wish him no good.

656.* Women and wine, game and deceit, make the wealth small and the wants great.

657. Words may show a man's wit, but actions his meaning.

658. Would you live with ease, do what you ought, and not what you please.

659. Would you persuade, speak of interest, not of reason.

660.* Write injuries in dust, benefits in marble.

661.* Write with the learned, pronounce with the vulgar.

662. Why does the blind man's wife paint herself?

663.* You can bear your own faults, and why not a fault in your wife.

664. You may be too cunning for one, but not for all.

665. You may delay, but time will not.

666. You may give a man an office, but you cannot give him discretion.

667. You may talk too much on the best subjects.

668. You may sometimes be much in the wrong, in owning your being in the right.

669.* Youth is pert and positive, age modest and doubting; so ears of corn when young and light, stand bolt upright, but hang their heads when weighty, full, and ripe.

670.* You will be careful, if you are wise; how you touch men's religion, or credit, or eyes.

A star preceding a saying signifies that it is to be taken as expressing two distinct and different thoughts.

COMMON SENSE

BY

THOMAS PAINE

ADDRESSED TO THE

INHABITANTS

OF

AMERICA,

On the following interesting

A new edition, with several additions in the body of the work. To which is added an APPENDIX; together with an address to the people called Quakers.

Man knows no Master save creating HEAVEN
Or those whom choice and common good ordain.

THOMSON.

PHILADELPHIA

Printed and sold by W. & T. Bradford, February 14, 1776.

MDCCLXXVI

PREPARED FOR PUBLICATION BY
HISTORIC PUBLISHING

San Antonio, Texas

Table of Contents

COMMON SENSE

INTRODUCTION.

PERHAPS the sentiments contained in the following pages, are not *yet* sufficiently fashionable to procure them general favor; a long habit of not thinking a thing *wrong*, gives it a superficial appearance of being *right*, and raises at first a formidable outcry in defense of custom. But the tumult soon subsides. Time makes more converts than reason.

As a long and violent abuse of power, is generally the Means of calling the right of it in question (and in Matters too which might never have been thought of, had not the Sufferers been aggravated into the inquiry) and as the King of England hath undertaken in his *own Right*, to support the Parliament in what he calls *Theirs*, and as the good people of this country are grievously oppressed by the combination, they have an undoubted privilege to inquire into the pretensions of both, and equally to reject the usurpation of either.

In the following sheets, the author hath studiously avoided every thing which is personal among ourselves. Compliments as well as censure to individuals make no part thereof. The wise, and the worthy, need not the triumph of a pamphlet; and those whose sentiments are injudicious, or unfriendly, will cease of themselves unless too much pains are bestowed upon their conversion.

The cause of America is in a great measure the cause of all mankind. Many circumstances hath, and will arise, which are not local, but universal, and through which the principles of all Lovers of Mankind are affected, and in the Event of which, their Affections are interested. The laying a Country desolate with Fire and Sword, declaring War against the natural rights of all Mankind, and extirpating the Defenders thereof from the Face of the Earth, is the Concern of every Man to whom Nature hath given the Power of feeling; of which Class, regardless of Party Censure, is the

AUTHOR

P.S. The Publication of this new Edition hath been delayed, with a View of taking notice (had it been necessary) of any Attempt to refute the Doctrine of Independance: As no Answer hath yet appeared, it is now presumed that none will, the Time needful for getting such a Performance ready for the Public being considerably past.

Who the Author of this Production is, is wholly unnecessary to the Public, as the Object for Attention is the *Doctrine itself*, not the *Man*. Yet it may not be unnecessary to say, That he is unconnected with any Party, and under no sort of Influence public or private, but the influence of reason and principle.

Philadelphia, February 14, 1776

OF THE ORIGIN AND DESIGN OF GOVERNMENT IN GENERAL, WITH CONCISE REMARKS ON THE ENGLISH CONSTITUTION.

SOME writers have so confounded society with government, as to leave little or no distinction between them; whereas they are not only different, but have different origins. Society is produced by our wants, and government by our wickedness; the former promotes our happiness *positively* by uniting our affections, the latter *negatively* by restraining our vices. The one encourages intercourse, the other creates distinctions. The first a patron, the last a punisher.

Society in every state is a blessing, but government even in its best state is but a necessary evil; in its worst state an intolerable one; for when we suffer, or are exposed to the same miseries *by a government*, which we might expect in a country *without government*, our calamity is heightened by reflecting that we furnish the means by which we suffer. Government, like dress, is the badge of lost innocence; the palaces of kings are built on the ruins of the bowers of paradise. For were the impulses of conscience clear, uniform, and irresistibly obeyed, man would need no other lawgiver; but that not being the case, he finds it necessary to surrender up a part of his property to furnish means for the protection of the rest; and this he is induced to do by the same prudence which in every other case advises him out of two evils to choose the least. *Wherefore*, security being the true design and end of government, it unanswerably follows that whatever *form* thereof appears most likely to ensure it to us, with the least expence and greatest benefit, is preferable to all others.

In order to gain a clear and just idea of the design and end of government, let us suppose a small number of persons settled in some sequestered part of the earth, unconnected with the rest, they will then represent the first peopling of any country, or of the world. In this state of natural liberty, society will be their first thought. A thousand motives will excite them thereto, the strength of one man is so unequal to his wants, and his mind so unfitted for perpetual solitude, that he is soon obliged to seek assistance and relief of another, who in his turn requires the same. Four or five united would be able to raise a tolerable dwelling in the midst of a wilderness, but *one* man might labour out of the common period of life without accomplishing anything; when he had felled his timber he could not remove it, nor erect it after it was removed; hunger in the meantime would urge him from his work, and every different want call him a different way. Disease, nay even misfortune would be death, for though neither might be mortal, yet either would disable him from living, and reduce him to a state in which he might rather be said to perish than to die.

Thus necessity, like a gravitating power, would soon form our newly arrived emigrants into society, the reciprocal blessings of which, would supersede, and render the obligations of law and government unnecessary while they remained perfectly just to each other; but as nothing but heaven is impregnable to vice, it will unavoidably happen, that in proportion as they surmount the first difficulties of emigration, which bound them together in a common cause, they will begin to relax in their duty and attachment to each other; and this remissness, will point out the necessity, of establishing some form of government to supply the defect of moral virtue.

Some convenient tree will afford them a State-House, under the branches of which, the whole colony may assemble to deliberate on public matters. It is more than probable that their first laws will have the title only of REGULATIONS, and be enforced by no other penalty than public disesteem. In this first parliament, every man, by natural right, will have a seat.

But as the colony increases, the public concerns will increase likewise, and the distance at which the members may be separated, will render it too inconvenient for all of them to meet on every occasion as at first, when their number was small, their habitations near, and the public concerns few and trifling. This will point out the convenience of their consenting to leave the legislative part to be managed by a select number chosen from the whole body, who are supposed to have the same concerns at stake which those who appointed them, and who will act in the same manner as the whole body would act were they present. If the colony continue increasing, it will become necessary to augment the number of the representatives, and that the interest of every part of the colony may be attended to, it will be found best to divide the whole into convenient parts, each part sending its proper number; and that the *elected* might never form to themselves an interest separate from the *electors*, prudence will point out the propriety of having elections often; because as the *elected* might by that means return and mix again with the general body of the *electors* in a few months, their fidelity to the public will be secured by the prudent reflexion of not making a rod for themselves. And as this frequent interchange will establish a common interest with every part of the community, they will mutually and naturally support each other, and on this (not on the unmeaning name of king) depends the *strength of government, and the happiness of the governed.*

Here then is the origin and rise of government; namely, a mode rendered necessary by the inability of moral virtue to govern the world; here too is the design and end of government, viz. freedom, and security. And however our eyes may be dazzled with show, or our ears deceived by sound; however prejudice may warp our wills, or interest darken our understanding, the simple voice of nature and of reason will say, it is right.

I draw my idea of the form of government from a principle in nature, which no art can overturn, viz. that the more simple any thing is, the less liable it is to be disordered; and the easier repaired when disordered; and with this maxim in view, I offer a few remarks on the so much boasted constitution of England. That it was noble for the dark and slavish times, in which it was erected, is granted. When the world was overrun with tyranny the least remove therefrom was a glorious rescue. But that it is imperfect, subject to convulsions, and incapable of producing what it seems to promise, is easily demonstrated.

Absolute governments (tho' the disgrace of human nature) have this advantage with them, that they are simple; if the people suffer, they know the head from which their suffering springs, know likewise the remedy, and are not bewildered by a variety of causes and cures. But the constitution of England is so exceedingly complex, that the nation may suffer for years together without being able to discover in which part the fault lies, some will say in one and some in another, and every political physician will advise a different medicine.

I know it is difficult to get over local or long standing prejudices, yet if we will suffer ourselves to examine the component parts of the English constitution, we shall find them to be the base remains of two ancient tyrannies, compounded with some new republican materials.

First.—The remains of monarchical tyranny in the person of the king.

Secondly.—The remains of aristocratical tyranny in the persons of the peers.

Thirdly.—The new republican materials, in the persons of the commons, on whose virtue depends the freedom of England.

The two first, by being hereditary, are independent of the people; wherefore in a *constitutional sense* they contribute nothing towards the freedom of the state.

To say that the constitution of England is a *union* of three powers reciprocally *checking* each other, is farcical, either the words have no meaning, or they are flat contradictions.

To say that the commons is a check upon the king, presupposes two things:

First.—That the king is not to be trusted without being looked after, or in other words, that a thirst for absolute power is the natural disease of monarchy.

Secondly.—That the commons, by being appointed for that purpose, are either wiser or more worthy of confidence than the crown.

But as the same constitution which gives the commons a power to check the king by withholding the supplies, gives afterwards the king a power to check the commons, by empowering him to reject their other bills; it again supposes that the king is wiser than those whom it has already supposed to be wiser than him. A mere absurdity!

There is something exceedingly ridiculous in the composition of monarchy; it first excludes a man from the means of information, yet empowers him to act in cases where the highest judgment is required. The state of a king shuts him from the world, yet the business of a king requires him to know it thoroughly; wherefore the different parts, by unnaturally opposing and destroying each other, prove the whole character to be absurd and useless.

Some writers have explained the English constitution thus; the king, say they, is one, the people another; the peers are an house in behalf of the king; the commons in behalf of the people; but this hath all the distinctions of a house divided against itself; and though the expressions be pleasantly arranged, yet when examined they appear idle and ambiguous; and it will always happen, that the nicest construction that words are capable of, when applied to the description of some thing which either cannot exist, or is too incomprehensible to be within the compass of description, will be words of sound only, and though they may amuse the ear, they cannot inform the mind, for this explanation includes a previous question, viz. *How came the king by a power which the people are afraid to trust, and always obliged to check?* Such a power could not be the gift of a wise people, neither can any power, *which needs checking*, be from God; yet the provision, which the constitution makes, supposes such a power to exist.

But the provision is unequal to the task; the means either cannot or will not accomplish the end, and the whole affair is a felo de se; for as the greater weight will always carry up the less, and as all the wheels of a machine are put in motion by one, it only remains to know which power in the constitution has the most weight, for that will govern; and though the others, or a part of them, may clog, or, as the phrase is, check the rapidity of its motion, yet so long as they cannot stop it, their endeavors will be ineffectual; the first moving power will at last have its way, and what it wants in speed is supplied by time.

That the crown is this overbearing part in the English constitution needs not be mentioned, and that it derives its whole consequence merely from being the giver of places and pensions is self-evident, wherefore, though we have been wise enough to shut and lock a door against absolute monarchy, we at the same time have been foolish enough to put the crown in possession of the key.

The prejudice of Englishmen, in favour of their own government by king, lords and commons, arises as much or more from national pride than reason. Individuals are undoubtedly safer in England than in some other countries, but the *will* of the king is as much the *law* of the land in Britain as in France, with this difference, that instead of proceeding directly from his mouth, it is handed to the people under the more formidable shape of an act of parliament. For the fate of Charles the first, hath only made kings more subtle—not more just.

Wherefore, laying aside all national pride and prejudice in favour of modes and forms, the plain truth is, that *it is wholly owing to the constitution of the people, and not to the constitution of the government* that the crown is not as oppressive in England as in Turkey.

An inquiry into the *constitutional errors* in the English form of government is at this time highly necessary, for as we are never in a proper condition of doing justice to others, while we continue under the influence of some leading partiality, so neither are we capable of doing it to ourselves while we remain fettered by any obstinate prejudice. And as a man, who is attached to a prostitute, is unfitted to choose or judge of a wife, so any prepossession in favour of a rotten constitution of government will disable us from discerning a good one.

OF MONARCHY AND HEREDITARY SUCCESSION.

MANKIND being originally equals in the order of creation, the equality could only be destroyed by some subsequent circumstance; the distinctions of rich, and poor, may in a great measure be accounted for, and that without having recourse to the harsh ill sounding names of oppression and avarice. Oppression is often the *consequence*, but seldom or never the *means* of riches; and though avarice will preserve a man from being necessitously poor, it generally makes him too timorous to be wealthy.

But there is another and greater distinction for which no truly natural or religious reason can be assigned, and that is, the distinction of men into KINGS and SUBJECTS. Male and female are the distinctions of nature, good and bad the distinctions of heaven; but how a race of men came into the world so exalted above the rest, and distinguished like some new species, is worth enquiring into, and whether they are the means of happiness or of misery to mankind.

In the early ages of the world, according to the scripture chronology, there were no kings; the consequence of which was there were no wars; it is the pride of kings which throw mankind into confusion. Holland without a king hath enjoyed more peace for this last century than any of the monarchial governments in Europe. Antiquity favors the same remark; for the quiet and rural lives of the first patriarchs hath a happy something in them, which vanishes away when we come to the history of Jewish royalty.

Government by kings was first introduced into the world by the Heathens, from whom the children of Israel copied the custom. It was the most prosperous invention the Devil ever set on foot for the promotion of idolatry. The Heathens paid divine honors to their deceased kings, and the christian world hath improved on the plan by doing the same to their living ones. How impious is the title of sacred majesty applied to a worm, who in the midst of his splendor is crumbling into dust!

As the exalting one man so greatly above the rest cannot be justified on the equal rights of nature, so neither can it be defended on the authority of scripture; for the will of the Almighty, as declared by Gideon and the prophet Samuel, expressly disapproves of government by kings. All anti-monarchical parts of scripture have been very smoothly glossed over in monarchical governments, but they undoubtedly merit the attention of countries which have their governments yet to form. "*Render unto Cæsar the things which are Cæsar's*" is the scripture doctrine of courts, yet it is no support of monarchical government, for the Jews at that time were without a king, and in a state of vassalage to the Romans.

Near three thousand years passed away from the Mosaic account of the creation, till the Jews under a national delusion requested a king. Till then their form of government (except in extraordinary cases, where the Almighty interposed) was a kind of republic administred by a judge and the elders of the tribes. Kings they had none, and it was held sinful to acknowledge any being under that title but the Lord of Hosts. And when a man seriously reflects on the idolatrous homage which is paid to the persons of Kings, he need not wonder, that the Almighty ever jealous of his honor, should disapprove of a form of government which so impiously invades the prerogative of heaven.

Monarchy is ranked in scripture as one of the sins of the Jews, for which a curse in reserve is denounced against them. The history of that transaction is worth attending to.

The children of Israel being oppressed by the Midianites, Gideon marched against them with a small army, and victory, thro' the divine interposition, decided in his favour. The Jews elate with success, and attributing it to the generalship of Gideon, proposed making him a king, saying, *Rule thou over us, thou and thy son and thy son's son.* Here was temptation in its fullest extent; not a kingdom only, but an hereditary one, but Gideon in the piety of his soul replied, *I will not rule over you, neither shall my son rule over you.* THE LORD SHALL RULE OVER YOU. Words need not be more explicit; Gideon doth not *decline* the honor, but denieth their right to give it; neither doth he compliment them with invented declarations of his thanks, but in the positive stile of a prophet charges them with disaffection to their proper Sovereign, the King of heaven.

About one hundred and thirty years after this, they fell again into the same error. The hankering which the Jews had for the idolatrous customs of the Heathens, is something exceedingly unaccountable; but so it was, that laying hold of the misconduct of Samuel's two sons, who were entrusted with some secular concerns, they came in an abrupt and clamorous manner to Samuel, saying, *Behold thou art old, and thy sons walk not in thy ways, now make us a king to judge us like all other nations.* And here we cannot but observe that their motives were bad, viz. that they might be *like* unto other nations, i.e. the Heathens, whereas their true glory laid in being as much *unlike* them as possible. *But the thing displeased Samuel when they said, Give us a king to judge us; and Samuel prayed unto the Lord, and the Lord said unto Samuel, Hearken unto the voice of the people in all that they say unto thee, for they have not rejected thee, but they have rejected me*, THAT I SHOULD NOT REIGN OVER THEM. *According to all the works which they have done since the day that I brought them up out of Egypt, even unto this day; wherewith they have forsaken me and served other Gods; so do they also unto thee. Now therefore hearken unto their voice, howbeit, protest solemnly unto them and shew them the manner of the king that shall reign over them, i.e.* not of any particular king, but the general manner of the kings of the earth, whom Israel was so eagerly copying after. And notwithstanding the great distance of time and difference of manners, the character is still in fashion. *And Samuel told all the words of the Lord unto the people, that asked of him a king. And he said, This shall be the manner of the king that shall reign over you; he will take your sons and appoint them for himself, for his chariots, and to be his horsemen, and some shall run before his chariots* (this description agrees with the present mode of impressing men) *and he will appoint him captains over thousands and captains over fifties, and will set them to ear his ground and to reap his harvest, and to make his instruments of war, and instruments of his chariots; and he will take your daughters to be confectionaries, and to be cooks and to be bakers* (this describes the expence and luxury as well as the oppression of kings) *and he will take your fields and your olive yards, even the best of them, and give them to his servants; and he will take the tenth of your feed, and of your vineyards, and give them to his officers and to his servants* (by which we see that bribery, corruption and favoritism are the standing vices of kings) *and he will take the tenth of your men servants, and your maid servants, and your goodliest young men and your asses, and put them to his work; and he will take the tenth of your sheep, and ye shall be his servants, and ye shall cry out in that day because of your king which ye shall have chosen,* AND THE LORD WILL NOT HEAR YOU IN THAT DAY. This accounts for the continuation of monarchy; neither do the characters of the few good kings which have lived since, either sanctify the title, or blot out the sinfulness of the origin; the high encomium given of David takes no notice of him *officially as a king*, but only as a *man* after God's own heart. *Nevertheless the People refused to obey the voice of Samuel, and they said, Nay, but we will have a king over us, that we may be like all the nations, and that our king may judge us, and go out before us, and fight our battles.* Samuel continued to reason with them, but to no purpose; he set before them their ingratitude, but all would not avail; and seeing them fully bent on their folly, he cried out, *I will call unto the Lord, and he shall send thunder and rain* (which then was a punishment, being in the time of wheat harvest) *that ye may perceive and see that your wickedness is great which ye have done in the sight of the Lord,* IN ASKING YOU A KING. *So Samuel called unto the Lord, and the Lord sent thunder and rain that day, and all the people greatly feared the Lord and Samuel. And all the people said unto Samuel, Pray for thy servants unto the Lord thy God that we die not, for* WE HAVE ADDED UNTO OUR SINS THIS EVIL, TO ASK A KING. These portions of scripture are direct and positive. They admit of no equivocal construction. That the Almighty hath here entered his protest against monarchical government is true, or the scripture is false. And a man hath good reason to believe that there is as much of king-craft, as priest-craft, in withholding the scripture from the public in Popish countries. For monarchy in every instance is the Popery of government.

To the evil of monarchy we have added that of hereditary succession; and as the first is a degradation and lessening of ourselves, so the second, claimed as a matter of right, is an insult and an imposition on posterity. For all men being originally equals, no *one* by *birth* could have a right to set up his own family in perpetual preference to all others for ever, and though himself might deserve *some* decent degree of honors of his cotemporaries, yet his descendants might be far too unworthy to inherit them. One of the strongest *natural* proofs of the folly of hereditary right in kings, is, that nature disapproves it, otherwise she would not so frequently turn it into ridicule by giving mankind an *ass for a lion.*

Secondly, as no man at first could possess any other public honors than were bestowed upon him, so the givers of those honors could have no power to give away the right of posterity, and though they might say "We choose you for *our* head," they could not, without manifest injustice to their children, say "that your children and your children's children shall reign over *ours* for ever." Because such an unwise, unjust, unnatural compact might (perhaps) in the next succession put them under the government of a rogue or a fool. Most wise men, in their private sentiments, have ever treated hereditary right with contempt; yet it is one of those evils, which when once established is not easily removed; many submit from fear, others from superstition, and the more powerful part shares with the king the plunder of the rest.

This is supposing the present race of kings in the world to have had an honorable origin; whereas it is more than probable, that could we take off the dark covering of antiquity, and trace them to their first rise, that we should find the first of them nothing better than the principal ruffian of some restless gang, whose savage manners or pre-eminence in subtility obtained him the title of chief among plunderers; and who by increasing in power, and extending his depredations, over-awed the quiet and defenceless to purchase their safety by frequent contributions. Yet his electors could have no idea of giving hereditary right to his descendants, because such a perpetual exclusion of themselves was incompatible with the free and unrestrained principles they professed to live by. Wherefore, hereditary succession in the early ages of monarchy could not take place as a matter of claim, but as something casual or complimental; but as few or no records were extant in those days, and traditional history stuffed with fables, it was very easy, after the lapse of a few generations, to trump up some superstitious tale, conveniently timed, Mahomet like, to cram hereditary right down the throats of the vulgar. Perhaps the disorders which threatened, or seemed to threaten, on the decease of a leader and the choice of a new one (for elections among ruffians could not be very orderly) induced many at first to favor hereditary pretensions; by which means it happened, as it hath happened since, that what at first was submitted to as a convenience, was afterwards claimed as a right.

England, since the conquest, hath known some few good monarchs, but groaned beneath a much larger number of bad ones; yet no man in his senses can say that their claim under William the Conqueror is a very honorable one. A French bastard landing with an armed banditti, and establishing himself king of England against the consent of the natives, is in plain terms a very paltry rascally original.—It certainly hath no divinity in it. However, it is needless to spend much time in exposing the folly of hereditary right; if there are any so weak as to believe it, let them promiscuously worship the ass and lion, and welcome. I shall neither copy their humility, nor disturb their devotion.

Yet I should be glad to ask how they suppose kings came at first? The question admits but of three answers, viz. either by lot, by election, or by usurpation. If the first king was taken by lot, it establishes a precedent for the next, which excludes hereditary succession. Saul was by lot, yet the succession was not hereditary, neither does it appear from that transaction there was any intention it ever should. If the first king of any country was by election, that likewise establishes a precedent for the next; for to say, that the *right* of all future generations is taken away, by the act of the first electors, in their choice not only of a king, but of a family of kings for ever, hath no parrallel in or out of scripture but the doctrine of original sin, which supposes the free will of all men lost in Adam; and from such comparison, and it will admit of no other, hereditary succession can derive no glory. For as in Adam all sinned, and as in the first electors all men obeyed; as in the one all mankind were subjected to Satan, and in the other to Sovereignty; as our innocence was lost in the first, and our authority in the last; and as both disable us from reassuming some former state and privilege, it unanswerably follows that original sin and hereditary succession are parellels. Dishonorable rank! Inglorious connexion! Yet the most subtile sophist cannot produce a juster simile.

As to usurpation, no man will be so hardy as to defend it; and that William the Conqueror was an usurper is a fact not to be contradicted. The plain truth is, that the antiquity of English monarchy will not bear looking into.

But it is not so much the absurdity as the evil of hereditary succession which concerns mankind. Did it ensure a race of good and wise men it would have the seal of divine authority, but as it opens a door to the *foolish*, the *wicked*, and the *improper*, it hath in it the nature of oppression. Men who look upon themselves born to reign, and others to obey, soon grow insolent; selected from the rest of mankind their minds are early poisoned by importance; and the world they act in differs so materially from the world at large, that they have but little opportunity of knowing its true interests, and when they succeed to the government are frequently the most ignorant and unfit of any throughout the dominions.

Another evil which attends hereditary succession is, that the throne is subject to be possessed by a minor at any age; all which time the regency, acting under the cover of a king, have every opportunity and inducement to betray their trust. The same national misfortune happens, when a king worn out with age and infirmity, enters the last stage of human weakness. In both these cases the public becomes a prey to every miscreant, who can tamper successfully with the follies either of age or infancy.

The most plausible plea, which hath ever been offered in favour of hereditary succession, is, that it preserves a nation from civil wars; and were this true, it would be weighty; whereas, it is the most barefaced falsity ever imposed upon mankind. The whole history of England disowns the fact. Thirty kings and two minors have reigned in that distracted kingdom since the conquest, in which time there have been (including the Revolution) no less than eight civil wars and nineteen rebellions. Wherefore instead of making for peace, it makes against it, and destroys the very foundation it seems to stand on.

The contest for monarchy and succession, between the houses of York and Lancaster, laid England in a scene of blood for many years. Twelve pitched battles, besides skirmishes and sieges, were fought between Henry and Edward. Twice was Henry prisoner to Edward, who in his turn was prisoner to Henry. And so uncertain is the fate of war and the temper of a nation, when nothing but personal matters are the ground of a quarrel, that Henry was taken in triumph from a prison to a palace, and Edward obliged to fly from a palace to a foreign land; yet, as sudden transitions of temper are seldom lasting, Henry in his turn was driven from the throne, and Edward recalled to succeed him. The parliament always following the strongest side.

This contest began in the reign of Henry the Sixth, and was not entirely extinguished till Henry the Seventh, in whom the families were united. Including a period of 67 years, viz. from 1422 to 1489.

In short, monarchy and succession have laid (not this or that kingdom only) but the world in blood and ashes. 'Tis a form of government which the word of God bears testimony against, and blood will attend it.

If we inquire into the business of a king, we shall find that in some countries they have none; and after sauntering away their lives without pleasure to themselves or advantage to the nation, withdraw from the scene, and leave their successors to tread the same idle round. In absolute monarchies the whole weight of business, civil and military, lies on the king; the children of Israel in their request for a king, urged this plea "that he may judge us, and go out before us and fight our battles." But in countries where he is neither a judge nor a general, as in England, a man would be puzzled to know what *is* his business.

The nearer any government approaches to a republic the less business there is for a king. It is somewhat difficult to find a proper name for the government of England. Sir William Meredith calls it a republic; but in its present state it is unworthy of the name, because the corrupt influence of the crown, by having all the places in its disposal, hath so effectually swallowed up the power, and eaten out the virtue of the house of commons (the republican part in the constitution) that the government of England is nearly as monarchical as that of France or Spain. Men fall out with names without understanding them. For it is the republican and not the monarchical part of the constitution of England which Englishmen glory in, viz. the liberty of choosing a house of commons from out of their own body—and it is easy to see that when republican virtue fails, slavery ensues. Why is the constitution of England sickly, but because monarchy hath poisoned the republic, the crown hath engrossed the commons?

In England a king hath little more to do than to make war and give away places; which in plain terms, is to impoverish the nation and set it together by the ears. A pretty business indeed for a man to be allowed eight hundred thousand sterling a year for, and worshipped into the bargain! Of more worth is one honest man to society and in the sight of God, than all the crowned ruffians that ever lived.

THOUGHTS ON THE PRESENT STATE OF AMERICAN AFFAIRS.

IN the following pages I offer nothing more than simple facts, plain arguments, and common sense; and have no other preliminaries to settle with the reader, than that he will divest himself of prejudice and prepossession, and suffer his reason and his feelings to determine for themselves; that he will put *on*, or rather that he will not put *off*, the true character of a man, and generously enlarge his views beyond the present day.

Volumes have been written on the subject of the struggle between England and America. Men of all ranks have embarked in the controversy, from different motives, and with various designs; but all have been ineffectual, and the period of debate is closed. Arms, as the last resource, decide the contest; the appeal was the choice of the king, and the continent hath accepted the challenge.

It hath been reported of the late Mr. Pelham (who tho' an able minister was not without his faults) that on his being attacked in the house of commons, on the score, that his measures were only of a temporary kind, replied "*they will last my time.*" Should a thought so fatal and unmanly possess the colonies in the present contest, the name of ancestors will be remembered by future generations with detestation.

The sun never shined on a cause of greater worth. 'Tis not the affair of a city, a country, a province, or a kingdom, but of a continent—of at least one eighth part of the habitable globe. 'Tis not the concern of a day, a year, or an age; posterity are virtually involved in the contest, and will be more or less affected, even to the end of time, by the proceedings now. Now is the seed time of continental union, faith and honor. The least fracture now will be like a name engraved with the point of a pin on the tender rind of a young oak; the wound will enlarge with the tree, and posterity read it in full grown characters.

By referring the matter from argument to arms, a new æra for politics is struck; a new method of thinking hath arisen. All plans, proposals, &c. prior to the nineteenth of April, *i.e.* to the commencement of hostilities, are like the almanacks of the last year; which, though proper then, are superseded and useless now. Whatever was advanced by the advocates on either side of the question then, terminated in one and the same point, viz. a union with Great-Britain; the only difference between the parties was the method of effecting it; the one proposing force, the other friendship; but it hath so far happened that the first hath failed, and the second hath withdrawn her influence.

As much hath been said of the advantages of reconciliation, which, like an agreeable dream, hath passed away and left us as we were, it is but right, that we should examine the contrary side of the argument, and inquire into some of the many material injuries which these colonies sustain, and always will sustain, by being connected with, and dependant on Great-Britain. To examine that connexion and dependance, on the principles of nature and common sense, to see what we have to trust to, if separated, and what we are to expect, if dependant.

I have heard it asserted by some, that as America hath flourished under her former connexion with Great-Britain, that the same connexion is necessary towards her future happiness, and will always have the same effect. Nothing can be more fallacious than this kind of argument. We may as well assert that because a child has thrived upon milk, that it is never to have meat, or that the first twenty years of our lives is to become a precedent for the next twenty. But even this is admitting more than is true, for I answer roundly, that America would have flourished as much, and probably much more, had no European power had any thing to do with her. The commerce, by which she hath enriched herself are the necessaries of life, and will always have a market while eating is the custom of Europe.

But she has protected us, say some. That she has engrossed us is true, and defended the continent at our expence as well as her own is admitted, and she would have defended Turkey from the same motive, viz. the sake of trade and dominion.

Alas, we have been long led away by ancient prejudices, and made large sacrifices to superstition. We have boasted the protection of Great-Britain, without considering, that her motive was *interest* not *attachment*; that she did not protect us from *our enemies* on *our account*, but from *her enemies* on *her own account*, from those who had no quarrel with us on any *other account*, and who will always be our enemies on the *same account*. Let Britain wave her pretensions to the continent, or the continent throw off the dependance, and we should be at peace with France and Spain were they at war with Britain. The miseries of Hanover last war ought to warn us against connexions.

It has lately been asserted in parliament, that the colonies have no relation to each other but through the parent country, *i.e.* that Pennsylvania and the Jerseys, and so on for the rest, are sister colonies by the way of England; this is certainly a very round-about way of proving relationship, but it is the nearest and only true way of proving enemyship, if I may so call it. France and Spain never were, nor perhaps ever will be our enemies as *Americans*, but as our being the *subjects of Great-Britain*.

But Britain is the parent country, say some. Then the more shame upon her conduct. Even brutes do not devour their young, nor savages make war upon their families; wherefore the assertion, if true, turns to her reproach; but it happens not to be true, or only partly so, and the phrase *parent* or *mother country* hath been jesuitically adopted by the king and his parasites, with a low papistical design of gaining an unfair bias on the credulous weakness of our minds. Europe, and not England, is the parent country of America. This new world hath been the asylum for the persecuted lovers of civil and religious liberty from *every part* of Europe. Hither have they fled, not from the tender embraces of the mother, but from the cruelty of the monster; and it is so far true of England, that the same tyranny which drove the first emigrants from home, pursues their descendants still.

In this extensive quarter of the globe, we forget the narrow limits of three hundred and sixty miles (the extent of England) and carry our friendship on a larger scale; we claim brotherhood with every European christian, and triumph in the generosity of the sentiment.

It is pleasant to observe by what regular gradations we surmount the force of local prejudice, as we enlarge our acquaintance with the world. A man born in any town in England divided into parishes, will naturally associate most with his fellow parishioners (because their interests in many cases will be common) and distinguish him by the name of *neighbour*; if he meet him but a few miles from home, he drops the narrow idea of a street, and salutes him by the name of *townsman*; if he travel out of the county, and meet him in any other, he forgets the minor divisions of street and town, and calls him *countryman*, i.e. *county-man*; but if in their foreign excursions they should associate in France or any other part of *Europe*, their local remembrance would be enlarged into that of *Englishmen*. And by a just parity of reasoning, all Europeans meeting in America, or any other quarter of the globe, are *countrymen*; for England, Holland, Germany, or Sweden, when compared with the whole, stand in the same places on the larger scale, which the divisions of street, town, and county do on the smaller ones; distinctions too limited for continental minds. Not one third of the inhabitants, even of this province, are of English descent. Wherefore I reprobate the phrase of parent or mother country applied to England only, as being false, selfish, narrow and ungenerous.

But admitting, that we were all of English descent, what does it amount to? Nothing. Britain, being now an open enemy, extinguishes every other name and title: And to say that reconciliation is our duty, is truly farcical. The first king of England, of the present line (William the Conqueror) was a Frenchman, and half the Peers of England are descendants from the same country; therefore, by the same method of reasoning, England ought to be governed by France.

Much hath been said of the united strength of Britain and the colonies, that in conjunction they might bid defiance to the world. But this is mere presumption; the fate of war is uncertain, neither do the expressions mean any thing; for this continent would never suffer itself to be drained of inhabitants, to support the British arms in either Asia, Africa, or Europe.

Besides what have we to do with setting the world at defiance? Our plan is commerce, and that, well attended to, will secure us the peace and friendship of all Europe; because, it is the interest of all Europe to have America a *free port.* Her trade will always be a protection, and her barrenness of gold and silver secure her from invaders.

I challenge the warmest advocate for reconciliation, to shew, a single advantage that this continent can reap, by being connected with Great Britain. I repeat the challenge, not a single advantage is derived. Our corn will fetch its price in any market in Europe, and our imported goods must be paid for buy them where we will.

But the injuries and disadvantages we sustain by that connection, are without number; and our duty to mankind at large, as well as to ourselves, instruct us to renounce the alliance: Because, any submission to, or dependance on Great-Britain, tends directly to involve this continent in European wars and quarrels; and sets us at variance with nations, who would otherwise seek our friendship, and against whom, we have neither anger nor complaint. As Europe is our market for trade, we ought to form no partial connection with any part of it. It is the true interest of America to steer clear of European contentions, which she never can do, while by her dependence on Britain, she is made the make-weight in the scale of British politics.

Europe is too thickly planted with kingdoms to be long at peace, and whenever a war breaks out between England and any foreign power, the trade of America goes to ruin, *because of her connection with Britain.* The next war may not turn out like the last, and should it not, the advocates for reconciliation now will be wishing for separation then, because, neutrality in that case, would be a safer convoy than a man of war. Every thing that is right or natural pleads for separation. The blood of the slain, the weeping voice of nature cries, 'TIS TIME TO PART. Even the distance at which the Almighty hath placed England and America, is a strong and natural proof, that the authority of the one, over the other, was never the design of Heaven. The time likewise at which the continent was discovered, adds weight to the argument, and the manner in which it was peopled encreases the force of it. The reformation was preceded by the discovery of America, as if the Almighty graciously meant to open a sanctuary to the persecuted in future years, when home should afford neither friendship nor safety.

The authority of Great-Britain over this continent, is a form of government, which sooner or later must have an end: And a serious mind can draw no true pleasure by looking forward, under the painful and positive conviction, that what he calls "the present constitution" is merely temporary. As parents, we can have no joy, knowing that *this government* is not sufficiently lasting to ensure any thing which we may bequeath to posterity: And by a plain method of argument, as we are running the next generation into debt, we ought to do the work of it, otherwise we use them meanly and pitifully. In order to discover the line of our duty rightly, we should take our children in our hand, and fix our station a few years farther into life; that eminence will present a prospect, which a few present fears and prejudices conceal from our sight.

Though I would carefully avoid giving unnecessary offence, yet I am inclined to believe, that all those who espouse the doctrine of reconciliation, may be included within the following descriptions. Interested men, who are not to be trusted; weak men, who *cannot* see; prejudiced men, who *will not* see; and a certain set of moderate men, who think better of the European world than it deserves; and this last class, by an ill-judged deliberation, will be the cause of more calamities to this continent, than all the other three.

It is the good fortune of many to live distant from the scene of sorrow; the evil is not sufficient brought to *their* doors to make *them* feel the precariousness with which all American property is possessed. But let our imaginations transport us for a few moments to Boston, that seat of wretchedness will teach us wisdom, and instruct us for ever to renounce a power in whom we can have no trust. The inhabitants of that unfortunate city, who but a few months ago were in ease and affluence, have now, no other alternative than to stay and starve, or turn out to beg. Endangered by the fire of their friends if they continue within the city, and plundered by the soldiery if they leave it. In their present condition they are prisoners without the hope of redemption, and in a general attack for their relief, they would be exposed to the fury of both armies.

Men of passive tempers look somewhat lightly over the offences of Britain, and, still hoping for the best, are apt to call out, "*Come, come, we shall be friends again, for all this.*" But examine the passions and feelings of mankind, Bring the doctrine of reconciliation to the touchstone of nature, and then tell me, whether you can hereafter love, honour, and faithfully serve the power that hath carried fire and sword into your land? If you cannot do all these, then are you only deceiving yourselves, and by your delay bringing ruin upon posterity. Your future connection with Britain, whom you can neither love nor honour, will be forced and unnatural, and being formed only on the plan of present convenience, will in a little time fall into a relapse more wretched than the first. But if you say, you can still pass the violations over, then I ask, Hath your house been burnt? Hath your property been destroyed before your face? Are your wife and children destitute of a bed to lie on, or bread to live on? Have you lost a parent or a child by their hands, and yourself the ruined and wretched survivor? If you have not, then are you not a judge of those who have. But if you have, and still can shake hands with the murderers, then are you unworthy of the name of husband, father, friend, or lover, and whatever may be your rank or title in life, you have the heart of a coward, and the spirit of a sycophant.

This is not inflaming or exaggerating matters, but trying them by those feelings and affections which nature justifies, and without which, we should be incapable of discharging the social duties of life, or enjoying the felicities of it. I mean not to exhibit horror for the purpose of provoking revenge, but to awaken us from fatal and unmanly slumbers, that we may pursue determinately some fixed object. It is not in the power of Britain or of Europe to conquer America, if she do not conquer herself by *delay* and *timidity*. The present winter is worth an age if rightly employed, but if lost or neglected, the whole continent will partake of the misfortune; and there is no punishment which that man will not deserve, be he who, or what, or where he will, that may be the means of sacrificing a season so precious and useful.

It is repugnant to reason, to the universal order of things to all examples from former ages, to suppose, that this continent can longer remain subject to any external power. The most sanguine in Britain does not think so. The utmost stretch of human wisdom cannot, at this time, compass a plan short of separation, which can promise the continent even a year's security. Reconciliation is *now* a fallacious dream. Nature hath deserted the connexion, and Art cannot supply her place. For, as Milton wisely expresses, "never can true reconcilement grow where wounds of deadly hate have pierced so deep."

Every quiet method for peace hath been ineffectual. Our prayers have been rejected with disdain; and only tended to convince us, that nothing flatters vanity, or confirms obstinacy in Kings more than repeated petitioning—and nothing hath contributed more than that very measure to make the Kings of Europe absolute: Witness Denmark and Sweden. Wherefore, since nothing but blows will do, for God's sake, let us come to a final separation, and not leave the next generation to be cutting throats, under the violated unmeaning names of parent and child.

To say, they will never attempt it again is idle and visionary, we thought so at the repeal of the stamp-act, yet a year or two undeceived us; as well may we suppose that nations, which have been once defeated, will never renew the quarrel.

As to government matters, it is not in the power of Britain to do this continent justice: The business of it will soon be too weighty, and intricate, to be managed with any tolerable degree of convenience, by a power, so distant from us, and so very ignorant of us; for if they cannot conquer us, they cannot govern us. To be always running three or four thousand miles with a tale or a petition, waiting four or five months for an answer, which when obtained requires five or six more to explain it in, will in a few years be looked upon as folly and childishness—There was a time when it was proper, and there is a proper time for it to cease.

Small islands not capable of protecting themselves, are the proper objects for kingdoms to take under their care; but there is something very absurd, in supposing a continent to be perpetually governed by an island. In no instance hath nature made the satellite larger than its primary planet, and as England and America, with respect to each other, reverses the common order of nature, it is evident they belong to different systems: England to Europe, America to itself.

I am not induced by motives of pride, party, or resentment to espouse the doctrine of separation and independance; I am clearly, positively, and conscientiously persuaded that it is the true interest of this continent to be so; that every thing short of *that* is mere patchwork, that it can afford no lasting felicity,—that it is leaving the sword to our children, and shrinking back at a time, when, a little more, a little farther, would have rendered this continent the glory of the earth.

As Britain hath not manifested the least inclination towards a compromise, we may be assured that no terms can be obtained worthy the acceptance of the continent, or any ways equal to the expence of blood and treasure we have been already put to.

The object, contended for, ought always to bear some just proportion to the expence. The removal of North, or the whole detestable junto, is a matter unworthy the millions we have expended. A temporary stoppage of trade, was an inconvenience, which would have sufficiently ballanced the repeal of all the acts complained of, had such repeals been obtained; but if the whole continent must take up arms, if every man must be a soldier, it is scarcely worth our while to fight against a contemptible ministry only. Dearly, dearly, do we pay for the repeal of the acts, if that is all we fight for; for in a just estimation, it is as great a folly to pay a Bunker-hill price for law, as for land. As I have always considered the independancy of this continent, as an event, which sooner or later must arrive, so from the late rapid progress of the continent to maturity, the event could not be far off. Wherefore, on the breaking out of hostilities, it was not worth the while to have disputed a matter, which time would have finally redressed, unless we meant to be in earnest; otherwise, it is like wasting an estate on a suit at law, to regulate the trespasses of a tenant, whose lease is just expiring. No man was a warmer wisher for reconciliation than myself, before the fatal nineteenth of April 1775, but the moment the event of that day was made known, I rejected the hardened, sullen tempered Pharaoh of England for ever; and disdain the wretch, that with the pretended title of FATHER OF HIS PEOPLE can unfeelingly hear of their slaughter, and composedly sleep with their blood upon his soul.

But admitting that matters were now made up, what would be the event? I answer, the ruin of the continent. And that for several reasons.

First. The powers of governing still remaining in the hands of the king, he will have a negative over the whole legislation of this continent. And as he hath shewn himself such an inveterate enemy to liberty, and discovered such a thirst for arbitrary power; is he, or is he not, a proper man to say to these colonies, "*You shall make no laws but what I please.*" And is there any inhabitant in America so ignorant, as not to know, that according to what is called the *present constitution*, that this continent can make no laws but what the king gives leave to; and is there any man so unwise, as not to see, that (considering what has happened) he will suffer no law to be made here, but such as suit *his* purpose. We may be as effectually enslaved by the want of laws in America, as by submitting to laws made for us in England. After matters are made up (as it is called) can there be any doubt, but the whole power of the crown will be exerted, to keep this continent as low and humble as possible? Instead of going forward we shall go backward, or be perpetually quarrelling or ridiculously petitioning.—We are already greater than the king wishes us to be, and will he not hereafter endeavour to make us less? To bring the matter to one point. Is the power who is jealous of our prosperity, a proper power to govern us? Whoever says *No* to this question is an *independant*, for independancy means no more, than, whether we shall make our own laws, or whether the king, the greatest enemy this continent hath, or can have, shall tell us "*there shall be no laws but such as I like.*"

But the king you will say has a negative in England; the people there can make no laws without his consent. In point of right and good order, there is something very ridiculous, that a youth of twenty-one (which hath often happened) shall say to several millions of people, older and wiser than himself, I forbid this or that act of yours to be law. But in this place I decline this sort of reply, though I will never cease to expose the absurdity of it, and only answer, that England being the King's residence, and America not so, makes quite another case. The king's negative *here* is ten times more dangerous and fatal than it can be in England, for *there* he will scarcely refuse his consent to a bill for putting England into as strong a state of defence as possible, and in America he would never suffer such a bill to be passed.

America is only a secondary object in the system of British politics, England consults the good of *this* country, no farther than it answers her *own* purpose. Wherefore, her own interest leads her to suppress the growth of *ours* in every case which doth not promote her advantage, or in the least interferes with it. A pretty state we should soon be in under such a second-hand government, considering what has happened! Men do not change from enemies to friends by the alteration of a name: And in order to shew that reconciliation *now* is a dangerous doctrine, I affirm, *that it would be policy in the king at this time, to repeal the acts for the sake of reinstating himself in the government of the provinces;* in order, that HE MAY ACCOMPLISH BY CRAFT AND SUBTILTY, IN THE LONG RUN, WHAT HE CANNOT DO BY FORCE AND VIOLENCE IN THE SHORT ONE. Reconciliation and ruin are nearly related.

Secondly. That as even the best terms, which we can expect to obtain, can amount to no more than a temporary expedient, or a kind of government by guardianship, which can last no longer than till the colonies come of age, so the general face and state of things, in the interim, will be unsettled and unpromising. Emigrants of property will not choose to come to a country whose form of government hangs but by a thread, and who is every day tottering on the brink of commotion and disturbance; and numbers of the present inhabitants would lay hold of the interval, to dispense of their effects, and quit the continent.

But the most powerful of all arguments, is, that nothing but independance, i.e. a continental form of government, can keep the peace of the continent and preserve it inviolate from civil wars. I dread the event of a reconciliation with Britain now, as it is more than probable, that it will be followed by a revolt somewhere or other, the consequences of which may be far more fatal than all the malice of Britain.

Thousands are already ruined by British barbarity; (thousands more will probably suffer the same fate) Those men have other feelings than us who have nothing suffered. All they *now* possess is liberty, what they before enjoyed is sacrificed to its service, and having nothing more to lose, they disdain submission. Besides, the general temper of the colonies, towards a British government, will be like that of a youth, who is nearly out of his time; they will care very little about her. And a government which cannot preserve the peace, is no government at all, and in that case we pay our money for nothing; and pray what is it that Britain can do, whose power will be wholly on paper, should a civil tumult break out the very day after reconciliation? I have heard some men say, many of whom I believe spoke without thinking, that they dreaded an independance, fearing that it would produce civil wars. It is but seldom that our first thoughts are truly correct, and that is the case here; for there are ten times more to dread from a patched up connexion than from independance. I make the sufferers case my own, and I protest, that were I driven from house and home, my property destroyed, and my circumstances ruined, that as man, sensible of injuries, I could never relish the doctrine of reconciliation, or consider myself bound thereby.

The colonies have manifested such a spirit of good order and obedience to continental government, as is sufficient to make every reasonable person easy and happy on that head. No man can assign the least pretence for his fears, on any other grounds, than such as are truly childish and ridiculous, viz. that one colony will be striving for superiority over another.

Where there are no distinctions there can be no superiority, perfect equality affords no temptation. The republics of Europe are all (and we may say always) in peace. Holland and Swisserland are without wars, foreign or domestic: Monarchical governments, it is true, are never long at rest; the crown itself is a temptation to enterprizing ruffians at *home*; and that degree of pride and insolence ever attendant on regal authority, swells into a rupture with foreign powers, in instances, where a republican government, by being formed on more natural principles, would negociate the mistake.

If there is any true cause of fear respecting independance, it is because no plan is yet laid down. Men do not see their way out—Wherefore, as an opening into that business, I offer the following hints; at the same time modestly affirming, that I have no other opinion of them myself, than that they may be the means of giving rise to something better. Could the straggling thoughts of individuals be collected, they would frequently form materials for wise and able men to improve into useful matter.

Let the assemblies be annual, with a President only. The representation more equal. Their business wholly domestic, and subject to the authority of a Continental Congress.

Let each colony be divided into six, eight, or ten, convenient districts, each district to send a proper number of delegates to Congress, so that each colony send at least thirty. The whole number in Congress will be at least 390. Each Congress to sit and to choose a president by the following method. When the delegates are met, let a colony be taken from the whole thirteen colonies by lot, after which, let the whole Congress choose (by ballot) a president from out of the delegates of *that* province. In the next Congress, let a colony be taken by lot from twelve only, omitting that colony from which the president was taken in the former Congress, and so proceeding on till the whole thirteen shall have had their proper rotation. And in order that nothing may pass into a law but what is satisfactorily just, not less than three fifths of the Congress to be called a majority.—He that will promote discord, under a government so equally formed as this, would have joined Lucifer in his revolt.

But as there is a peculiar delicacy, from whom, or in what manner, this business must first arise, and as it seems most agreeable and consistent that it should come from some intermediate body between the governed and the governors, that is, between the Congress and the people, let a CONTINENTAL CONFERENCE be held, in the following manner, and for the following purpose.

A committee of twenty-six members of Congress, viz. two for each colony. Two members from each House of Assembly, or Provincial Convention; and five representatives of the people at large, to be chosen in the capital city or town of each province, for, and in behalf of the whole province, by as many qualified voters as shall think proper to attend from all parts of the province for that purpose; or, if more convenient, the representatives may be chosen in two or three of the most populous parts thereof. In this conference, thus assembled, will be united, the two grand principles of business, *knowledge* and *power*. The members of Congress, Assemblies, or Conventions, by having had experience in national concerns, will be able and useful counsellors, and the whole, being impowered by the people, will have a truly legal authority.

The conferring members being met, let their business be to frame a CONTINENTAL CHARTER, or Charter of the United Colonies; (answering to what is called the Magna Charta of England) fixing the number and manner of choosing members of Congress, members of Assembly, with their date of sitting, and drawing the line of business and jurisdiction between them: (Always remembering, that our strength is continental, not provincial:) Securing freedom and property to all men, and above all things, the free exercise of religion, according to the dictates of conscience; with such other matter as is necessary for a charter to contain. Immediately after which, the said Conference to dissolve, and the bodies which shall be chosen comformable to the said charter, to be the legislators and governors of this continent for the time being: Whose peace and happiness, may God preserve, Amen.

Should any body of men be hereafter delegated for this or some similar purpose, I offer them the following extracts from that wise observer on governments *Dragonetti*. "The science" says he "of the politician consists in fixing the true point of happiness and freedom. Those men would deserve the gratitude of ages, who should discover a mode of government that contained the greatest sum of individual happiness, with the least national expense.

Dragonetti on virtue and rewards."

But where says some is the King of America? I'll tell you Friend, he reigns above, and doth not make havoc of mankind like the Royal Brute of Britain. Yet that we may not appear to be defective even in earthly honors, let a day be solemnly set apart for proclaiming the charter; let it be brought forth placed on the divine law, the word of God; let a crown be placed thereon, by which the world may know, that so far as we approve of monarchy, that in America THE LAW IS KING. For as in absolute governments the King is law, so in free countries the law *ought* to be King; and there ought to be no other. But lest any ill use should afterwards arise, let the crown at the conclusion of the ceremony be demolished, and scattered among the people whose right it is.

A government of our own is our natural right: And when a man seriously reflects on the precariousness of human affairs, he will become convinced, that it is infinitely wiser and safer, to form a constitution of our own in a cool deliberate manner, while we have it in our power, than to trust such an interesting event to time and chance. If we omit it now, some Massanello [1] may hereafter arise, who laying hold of popular disquietudes, may collect together the desperate and the discontented, and by assuming to themselves the powers of government, may sweep away the liberties of the continent like a deluge. Should the government of America return again into the hands of Britain, the tottering situation of things, will be a temptation for some desperate adventurer to try his fortune; and in such a case, what relief can Britain give? Ere she could hear the news, the fatal business might be done; and ourselves suffering like the wretched Britons under the oppression of the Conqueror. Ye that oppose independance now, ye know not what ye do; ye are opening a door to eternal tyranny, by keeping vacant the seat of government. There are thousands, and tens of thousands, who would think it glorious to expel from the continent, that barbarous and hellish power, which hath stirred up the Indians and Negroes to destroy us, the cruelty hath a double guilt, it is dealing brutally by us, and treacherously by them.

[1] Thomas Anello, otherwise Massanello, a fisherman of Naples, who after spiriting up his countrymen in the public market place, against the oppressions of the Spaniards, to whom the place was then subject, prompted them to revolt, and in the space of a day became king.

To talk of friendship with those in whom our reason forbids us to have faith, and our affections wounded through a thousand pores instruct us to detest, is madness and folly. Every day wears out the little remains of kindred between us and them, and can there be any reason to hope, that as the relationship expires, the affection will increase, or that we shall agree better, when we have ten times more and greater concerns to quarrel over than ever?

Ye that tell us of harmony and reconciliation, can ye restore to us the time that is past? Can ye give to prostitution its former innocence? Neither can ye reconcile Britain and America. The last cord now is broken, the people of England are presenting addresses against us. There are injuries which nature cannot forgive; she would cease to be nature if she did. As well can the lover forgive the ravisher of his mistress, as the continent forgive the murders of Britain. The Almighty hath implanted in us these unextinguishable feelings for good and wise purposes. They are the guardians of his image in our hearts. They distinguish us from the herd of common animals. The social compact would dissolve, and justice be extirpated the earth, or have only a casual existence were we callous to the touches of affection. The robber, and the murderer, would often escape unpunished, did not the injuries which our tempers sustain, provoke us into justice.

O ye that love mankind! Ye that dare oppose, not only the tyranny, but the tyrant, stand forth! Every spot of the old world is overrun with oppression. Freedom hath been hunted round the globe. Asia, and Africa, have long expelled her—Europe regards her like a stranger, and England hath given her warning to depart. O! receive the fugitive, and prepare in time an asylum for mankind.

OF THE PRESENT ABILITY OF AMERICA, WITH SOME MISCELLANEOUS REFLEXIONS.

I HAVE never met with a man, either in England or America, who hath not confessed his opinion, that a separation between the countries, would take place one time or other: And there is no instance, in which we have shewn less judgment, than in endeavouring to describe, what we call, the ripeness or fitness of the Continent for independance.

As all men allow the measure, and vary only in their opinion of the time, let us, in order to remove mistakes, take a general survey of things, and endeavour, if possible, to find out the *very* time. But we need not go far, the inquiry ceases at once, for, the *time hath found us*. The general concurrence, the glorious union of all things prove the fact.

It is not in numbers, but in unity, that our great strength lies; yet our present numbers are sufficient to repel the force of all the world. The Continent hath, at this time, the largest body of armed and disciplined men of any power under Heaven; and is just arrived at that pitch of strength, in which no single colony is able to support itself, and the whole, when united, can accomplish the matter, and either more, or, less than this, might be fatal in its effects. Our land force is already sufficient, and as to naval affairs, we cannot be insensible, that Britain would never suffer an American man of war to be built, while the continent remained in her hands. Wherefore, we should be no forwarder an hundred years hence in that branch, than we are now; but the truth is, we should be less so, because the timber of the country is every day diminishing, and that, which will remain at last, will be far off and difficult to procure.

Were the continent crowded with inhabitants, her sufferings under the present circumstances would be intolerable. The more sea port towns we had, the more should we have both to defend and to lose. Our present numbers are so happily proportioned to our wants, that no man need be idle. The diminution of trade affords an army, and the necessities of an army create a new trade.

Debts we have none; and whatever we may contract on this account will serve as a glorious memento of our virtue. Can we but leave posterity with a settled form of government, an independant constitution of its own, the purchase at any price will be cheap. But to expend millions for the sake of getting a few vile acts repealed, and routing the present ministry only, is unworthy the charge, and is using posterity with the utmost cruelty; because it is leaving them the great work to do, and a debt upon their backs, from which they derive no advantage. Such a thought is unworthy a man of honor, and is the true characteristic of a narrow heart and a pedling politician.

The debt we may contract doth not deserve our regard if the work be but accomplished. No nation ought to be without a debt. A national debt is a national bond; and when it bears no interest, is in no case a grievance. Britain is oppressed with a debt of upwards of one hundred and forty millions sterling, for which she pays upwards of four millions interest. And as a compensation for her debt, she has a large navy; America is without a debt, and without a navy; yet for the twentieth part of the English national debt, could have a navy as large again. The navy of England is not worth, at this time, more than three millions and an half sterling.

The first and second editions of this pamphlet were published without the following calculations, which are now given as a proof that the above estimation of the navy is just. *See Entic's naval history, intro.* page 56.

The charge of building a ship of each rate, and furnishing her with masts, yards, sails and rigging, together with a proportion of eight months boatswain's and carpenter's sea-stores, as calculated by Mr. Burchett, Secretary to the navy.

		£ [pounds sterling]
For a ship of 100 guns	=	35,553
90	=	29,886
80	=	23,638
70	=	17,785
60	=	14,197
50	=	10,606
40	=	7,558
30	=	5,846

20 = 3,710

And from hence it is easy to sum up the value, or cost rather, of the whole British navy, which in the year 1757, when it was at its greatest glory consisted of the following ships and guns:

Ships.	Guns.	Cost of one.	Cost of all.
		Cost in £ [pounds sterling]	
6	100	35,553	213,318
12	90	29,886	358,632
12	80	23,638	283,656
43	70	17,785	764,755
35	60	14,197	496,895
40	50	10,606	424,240
45	40	7,558	340,110
58	20	3,710	215,180

85	Sloops, bombs and fireships, one with another, at	2,000	170,000

	Cost		3,266,786
	Remains for Guns		233,214

			3,500,000

No country on the globe is so happily situated, or so internally capable of raising a fleet as America. Tar, timber, iron, and cordage are her natural produce. We need go abroad for nothing. Whereas the Dutch, who make large profits by hiring out their ships of war to the Spaniards and Portuguese, are obliged to import most of the materials they use. We ought to view the building a fleet as an article of commerce, it being the natural manufactory of this country. It is the best money we can lay out. A navy when finished is worth more than it cost. And is that nice point in national policy, in which commerce and protection are united. Let us build; if we want them not, we can sell; and by that means replace our paper currency with ready gold and silver.

In point of manning a fleet, people in general run into great errors; it is not necessary that one fourth part should be sailors.

The Terrible privateer, Captain Death, stood the hottest engagement of any ship last war, yet had not twenty sailors on board, though her complement of men was upwards of two hundred. A few able and social sailors will soon instruct a sufficient number of active landmen in the common work of a ship. Wherefore, we never can be more capable to begin on maritime matters than now, while our timber is standing, our fisheries blocked up, and our sailors and shipwrights out of employ. Men of war, of seventy and eighty guns were built forty years ago in New-England, and why not the same now? Ship-building is America's greatest pride, and in which, she will in time excel the whole world. The great empires of the east are mostly inland, and consequently excluded from the possibility of rivalling her. Africa is in a state of barbarism; and no power in Europe, hath either such an extent of coast, or such an internal supply of materials. Where nature hath given the one, she has withheld the other; to America only hath she been liberal of both. The vast empire of Russia is almost shut out from the sea; wherefore, her boundless forests, her tar, iron, and cordage are only articles of commerce.

In point of safety, ought we to be without a fleet? We are not the little people now, which we were sixty years ago; at that time we might have trusted our property in the streets, or fields rather; and slept securely without locks or bolts to our doors or windows. The case now is altered, and our methods of defence, ought to improve with our increase of property. A common pirate, twelve months ago, might have come up the Delaware, and laid the city of Philadelphia under instant contribution, for what sum he pleased; and the same might have happened to other places. Nay, any daring fellow, in a brig of fourteen or sixteen guns, might have robbed the whole Continent, and carried off half a million of money. These are circumstances which demand our attention, and point out the necessity of naval protection.

Some, perhaps, will say, that after we have made it up with Britain, she will protect us. Can we be so unwise as to mean, that she shall keep a navy in our harbours for that purpose? Common sense will tell us, that the power which hath endeavoured to subdue us, is of all others, the most improper to defend us. Conquest may be effected under the pretence of friendship; and ourselves, after a long and brave resistance, be at last cheated into slavery. And if her ships are not to be admitted into our harbours, I would ask, how is she to protect us? A navy three or four thousand miles off can be of little use, and on sudden emergencies, none at all. Wherefore, if we must hereafter protect ourselves, why not do it for ourselves? Why do it for another?

The English list of ships of war, is long and formidable, but not a tenth part of them are at any one time fit for service, numbers of them not in being; yet their names are pompously continued in the list, if only a plank be left of the ship: and not a fifth part, of such as are fit for service, can be spared on any one station at one time. The East and West Indies, Mediterranean, Africa, and other parts over which Britain extends her claim, make large demands upon her navy. From a mixture of prejudice and inattention, we have contracted a false notion respecting the navy of England, and have talked as if we should have the whole of it to encounter at once, and for that reason, supposed, that we must have one as large; which not being instantly practicable, have been made use of by a set of disguised Tories to discourage our beginning thereon. Nothing can be farther from truth than this; for if America had only a twentieth part of the naval force of Britain, she would be by far an over match for her; because, as we neither have, nor claim any foreign dominion, our whole force would be employed on our own coast, where we should, in the long run, have two to one the advantage of those who had three or four thousand miles to sail over, before they could attack us, and the same distance to return in order to refit and recruit. And although Britain by her fleet, hath a check over our trade to

Europe, we have as large a one over her trade to the West-Indies, which, by laying in the neighbourhood of the Continent, is entirely at its mercy.

Some method might be fallen on to keep up a naval force in time of peace, if we should not judge it necessary to support a constant navy. If premiums were to be given to merchants, to build and employ in their service ships mounted with twenty, thirty, forty or fifty guns, (the premiums to be in proportion to the loss of bulk to the merchants) fifty or sixty of those ships, with a few guardships on constant duty, would keep up a sufficient navy, and that without burdening ourselves with the evil so loudly complained of in England, of suffering their fleet, in time of peace to lie rotting in the docks. To unite the sinews of commerce and defense is sound policy; for when our strength and our riches play into each other's hand, we need fear no external enemy.

In almost every article of defense we abound. Hemp flourishes even to rankness, so that we need not want cordage. Our iron is superior to that of other countries. Our small arms equal to any in the world. Cannon we can cast at pleasure. Saltpetre and gunpowder we are every day producing. Our knowledge is hourly improving. Resolution is our inherent character, and courage hath never yet forsaken us. Wherefore, what is it that we want? Why is it that we hesitate? From Britain we can expect nothing but ruin. If she is once admitted to the government of America again, this Continent will not be worth living in. Jealousies will be always arising; insurrections will be constantly happening; and who will go forth to quell them? Who will venture his life to reduce his own countrymen to a foreign obedience? The difference between Pennsylvania and Connecticut, respecting some unlocated lands, shews the insignificance of a British government, and fully proves, that nothing but Continental authority can regulate Continental matters.

Another reason why the present time is preferable to all others, is, that the fewer our numbers are, the more land there is yet unoccupied, which instead of being lavished by the king on his worthless dependants, may be hereafter applied, not only to the discharge of the present debt, but to the constant support of government. No nation under heaven hath such an advantage as this.

The infant state of the Colonies, as it is called, so far from being against, is an argument in favour of independance. We are sufficiently numerous, and were we more so, we might be less united. It is a matter worthy of observation, that the more a country is peopled, the smaller their armies are. In military numbers, the ancients far exceeded the moderns: and the reason is evident. For trade being the consequence of population, men become too much absorbed thereby to attend to anything else. Commerce diminishes the spirit, both of patriotism and military defence. And history sufficiently informs us, that the bravest achievements were always accomplished in the non-age of a nation. With the increase of commerce, England hath lost its spirit. The city of London, notwithstanding its numbers, submits to continued insults with the patience of a coward. The more men have to lose, the less willing are they to venture. The rich are in general slaves to fear, and submit to courtly power with the trembling duplicity of a Spaniel.

Youth is the seed time of good habits, as well in nations as in individuals. It might be difficult, if not impossible, to form the Continent into one government half a century hence. The vast variety of interests, occasioned by an increase of trade and population, would create confusion. Colony would be against colony. Each being able might scorn each other's assistance: and while the proud and foolish gloried in their little distinctions, the wise would lament, that the union had not been formed before. Wherefore, the *present time* is the *true time* for establishing it. The intimacy which is contracted in infancy, and the friendship which is formed in misfortune, are, of all others, the most lasting and unalterable. Our present union is marked with both these characters: we are young and we have been distressed; but our concord hath withstood our troubles, and fixes a memorable area for posterity to glory in.

The present time, likewise, is that peculiar time, which never happens to a nation but once, viz. the time of forming itself into a government. Most nations have let slip the opportunity, and by that means have been compelled to receive laws from their conquerors, instead of making laws for themselves. First, they had a king, and then a form of government; whereas, the articles or charter of government, should be formed first, and men delegated to execute them afterward: but from the errors of other nations, let us learn wisdom, and lay hold of the present opportunity—*To begin government at the right end.*

When William the Conqueror subdued England, he gave them law at the point of the sword; and until we consent, that the seat of government, in America, be legally and authoritatively occupied, we shall be in danger of having it filled by some fortunate ruffian, who may treat us in the same manner, and then, where will be our freedom? where our property?

As to religion, I hold it to be the indispensable duty of all government, to protect all conscientious professors thereof, and I know of no other business which government hath to do therewith. Let a man throw aside that narrowness of soul, that selfishness of principle, which the niggards of all professions are so unwilling to part with, and he will be at once delivered of his fears on that head. Suspicion is the companion of mean souls, and the bane of all good society. For myself, I fully and conscientiously believe, that it is the will of the Almighty, that there should be diversity of religious opinions among us: It affords a larger field for our Christian kindness. Were we all of one way of thinking, our religious dispositions would want matter for probation; and on this liberal principle, I look on the various denominations among us, to be like children of the same family, differing only, in what is called, their Christian names.

In page forty, I threw out a few thoughts on the propriety of a Continental Charter, (for I only presume to offer hints, not plans) and in this place, I take the liberty of re-mentioning the subject, by observing, that a charter is to be understood as a bond of solemn obligation, which the whole enters into, to support the right of every separate part, whether of religion, personal freedom, or property. A firm bargain and a right reckoning make long friends.

In a former page I likewise mentioned the necessity of a large and equal representation; and there is no political matter which more deserves our attention. A small number of electors, or a small number of representatives, are equally dangerous. But if the number of the representatives be not only small, but unequal, the danger is increased. As an instance of this, I mention the following; when the Associators petition was before the House of Assembly of Pennsylvania; twenty-eight members only were present, all the Bucks county members, being eight, voted against it, and had seven of the Chester members done the same, this whole province had been governed by two counties only, and this danger it is always exposed to. The unwarrantable stretch likewise, which that house made in their last sitting, to gain an undue authority over the delegates of that province, ought to warn the people at large, how they trust power out of their own hands. A set of instructions for the Delegates were put together, which in point of sense and business would have dishonoured a schoolboy, and after being approved by a *few*, a *very few* without doors, were carried into the House, and there passed *in behalf of the whole colony*; whereas, did the whole colony know, with what ill-will that House hath entered on some necessary public measures, they would not hesitate a moment to think them unworthy of such a trust.

Immediate necessity makes many things convenient, which if continued would grow into oppressions. Expedience and right are different things. When the calamities of America required a consultation, there was no method so ready, or at that time so proper, as to appoint persons from the several Houses of Assembly for that purpose; and the wisdom with which they have proceeded hath preserved this continent from ruin. But as it is more than probable that we shall never be without a CONGRESS, every well wisher to good order, must own, that the mode for choosing members of that body, deserves consideration. And I put it as a question to those, who make a study of mankind, whether *representation and election* is not too great a power for one and the same body of men to possess? When we are planning for posterity, we ought to remember, that virtue is not hereditary.

It is from our enemies that we often gain excellent maxims, and are frequently surprised into reason by their mistakes. Mr. Cornwall (one of the Lords of the Treasury) treated the petition of the New-York Assembly with contempt, because *that* House, he said, consisted but of twenty-six members, which trifling number, he argued, could not with decency be put for the whole. We thank him for his involuntary honesty. [1]

[1] Those who would fully understand of what great consequence a large and equal representation is to a state, should read Burgh's political disquisitions.

TO CONCLUDE, however strange it may appear to some, or however unwilling they may be to think so, matters not, but many strong and striking reasons may be given, to shew, that nothing can settle our affairs so expeditiously as an open and determined declaration for independance. Some of which are,

First.—It is the custom of nations, when any two are at war, for some other powers, not engaged in the quarrel, to step in as mediators, and bring about the preliminaries of a peace: but while America calls herself the Subject of Great-Britain, no power, however well disposed she may be, can offer her mediation. Wherefore, in our present state we may quarrel on for ever.

Secondly.—It is unreasonable to suppose, that France or Spain will give us any kind of assistance, if we mean only, to make use of that assistance for the purpose of repairing the breach, and strengthening the connection between Britain and America; because, those powers would be sufferers by the consequences.

Thirdly.—While we profess ourselves the subjects of Britain, we must, in the eye of foreign nations, be considered as rebels. The precedent is somewhat dangerous to *their peace*, for men to be in arms under the name of subjects; we, on the spot, can solve the paradox: but to unite resistance and subjection, requires an idea much too refined for common understanding.

Fourthly.—Were a manifesto to be published, and despatched to foreign courts, setting forth the miseries we have endured, and the peaceable methods we have ineffectually used for redress; declaring, at the same time, that not being able, any longer, to live happily or safely under the cruel disposition of the British court, we had been driven to the necessity of breaking off all connections with her; at the same time, assuring all such courts of our peaceable disposition towards them, and of our desire of entering into trade with them: Such a memorial would produce more good effects to this Continent, than if a ship were freighted with petitions to Britain.

Under our present denomination of British subjects, we can neither be received nor heard abroad: The custom of all courts is against us, and will be so, until, by an independance, we take rank with other nations.

These proceedings may at first appear strange and difficult; but, like all other steps which we have already passed over, will in a little time become familiar and agreeable; and, until an independance is declared, the Continent will feel itself like a man who continues putting off some unpleasant business from day to day, yet knows it must be done, hates to set about it, wishes it over, and is continually haunted with the thoughts of its necessity.

APPENDIX.

SINCE the publication of the first edition of this pamphlet, or rather, on the same day on which it came out, the King's Speech made its appearance in this city. Had the spirit of prophecy directed the birth of this production, it could not have brought it forth, at a more seasonable juncture, or a more necessary time. The bloody mindedness of the one, shew the necessity of pursuing the doctrine of the other. Men read by way of revenge. And the Speech, instead of terrifying, prepared a way for the manly principles of Independance.

Ceremony, and even, silence, from whatever motive they may arise, have a hurtful tendency, when they give the least degree of countenance to base and wicked performances; wherefore, if this maxim be admitted, it naturally follows, that the King's Speech, as being a piece of finished villainy, deserved, and still deserves, a general execration both by the Congress and the people. Yet, as the domestic tranquillity of a nation, depends greatly, on the *chastity* of what may properly be called NATIONAL MANNERS, it is often better, to pass some things over in silent disdain, than to make use of such new methods of dislike, as might introduce the least innovation, on that guardian of our peace and safety. And, perhaps, it is chiefly owing to this prudent delicacy, that the King's Speech, hath not, before now, suffered a public execution. The Speech if it may be called one, is nothing better than a wilful audacious libel against the truth, the common good, and the existence of mankind; and is a formal and pompous method of offering up human sacrifices to the pride of tyrants. But this general massacre of mankind, is one of the privileges, and the certain consequence of Kings; for as nature knows them *not*, they know *not her*, and although they are beings of our *own* creating, they know not *us*, and are become the gods of their creators. The Speech hath one good quality, which is, that it is not calculated to deceive, neither can we, even if we would, be deceived by it. Brutality and tyranny appear on the face of it. It leaves us at no loss: And every line convinces, even in the moment of reading, that He, who hunts the woods for prey, the naked and untutored Indian, is less a Savage than the King of Britain.

Sir John Dalrymple, the putative father of a whining jesuitical piece, fallaciously called, "*The Address of the people of* ENGLAND *to the inhabitants of* AMERICA," hath, perhaps, from a vain supposition, that the people *here* were to be frightened at the pomp and description of a king, given, (though very unwisely on his part) the real character of the present one: "But" says this writer, "if you are inclined to pay compliments to an administration, which we do not complain of," (meaning the Marquis of Rockingham's at the repeal of the Stamp Act) "it is very unfair in you to withhold them from that prince, *by whose* NOD ALONE *they were permitted to do any thing*." This is toryism with a witness! Here is idolatry even without a mask: And he who can calmly hear, and digest such doctrine, hath forfeited his claim to rationality—an apostate from the order of manhood; and ought to be considered—as one, who hath not only given up the proper dignity of man, but sunk himself beneath the rank of animals, and contemptibly crawls through the world like a worm.

However, it matters very little now, what the king of England either says or does; he hath wickedly broken through every moral and human obligation, trampled nature and conscience beneath his feet; and by a steady and constitutional spirit of insolence and cruelty, procured for himself an universal hatred. It is *now* the interest of America to provide for herself. She hath already a large and young family, whom it is more her duty to take care of, than to be granting away her property, to support a power who is become a reproach to the names of men and christians—YE, whose office it is to watch over the morals of a nation, of whatsoever sect or denomination ye are of, as well as ye, who are more immediately the guardians of the public liberty, if ye wish to preserve your native country uncontaminated by European corruption, ye must in secret wish a separation—But leaving the moral part to private reflection, I shall chiefly confine my farther remarks to the following heads.

First. That it is the interest of America to be separated from Britain.

Secondly. Which is the easiest and most practicable plan, RECONCILIATION or INDEPENDANCE? with some occasional remarks.

In support of the first, I could, if I judged it proper, produce the opinion of some of the ablest and most experienced men on this continent; and whose sentiments, on that head, are not yet publicly known. It is in reality a self-evident position: For no nation in a state of foreign dependance, limited in its commerce, and cramped and fettered in its legislative powers, can ever arrive at any material eminence. America doth not yet know what opulence is; and although the progress which she hath made stands unparalleled in the history of other nations, it is but childhood, compared with what she would be capable of arriving at, had she, as she ought to have, the legislative powers in her own hands. England is, at this time, proudly coveting what would do her no good, were she to accomplish it; and the Continent hesitating on a matter, which will be her final ruin if neglected. It is the commerce and not the conquest of America, by which England is to be benefited, and that would in a great measure continue, were the countries as independant of each other as France and Spain; because in many articles, neither can go to a better market. But it is the independance of this country of Britain or any other, which is now the main and only object worthy of contention, and which, like all other truths discovered by necessity, will appear clearer and stronger every day.

First. Because it will come to that one time or other.

Secondly. Because, the longer it is delayed the harder it will be to accomplish.

I have frequently amused myself both in public and private companies, with silently remarking, the specious errors of those who speak without reflecting. And among the many which I have heard, the following seems the most general, viz. that had this rupture happened forty or fifty years hence, instead of *now*, the Continent would have been more able to have shaken off the dependance. To which I reply, that our military ability, *at this time*, arises from the experience gained in the last war, and which in forty or fifty years time, would have been totally extinct. The Continent, would not, by that time, have had a General, or even a military officer left; and we, or those who may succeed us, would have been as ignorant of martial matters as the ancient Indians: And this single position, closely attended to, will unanswerably prove, that the present time is preferable to all others. The argument turns thus—at the conclusion of the last war, we had experience, but wanted numbers; and forty or fifty years hence, we should have numbers, without experience; wherefore, the proper point of time, must be some particular point between the two extremes, in which a sufficiency of the former remains, and a proper increase of the latter is obtained: And that point of time is the present time.

The reader will pardon this digression, as it does not properly come under the head I first set out with, and to which I again return by the following position, viz.

Should affairs be patched up with Britain, and she to remain the governing and sovereign power of America, (which, as matters are now circumstanced, is giving up the point intirely) we shall deprive ourselves of the very means of sinking the debt we have, or may contract. The value of the back lands which some of the provinces are clandestinely deprived of, by the unjust extention of the limits of Canada, valued only at five pounds sterling per hundred acres, amount to upwards of twenty-five millions, Pennsylvania currency; and the quit-rents at one penny sterling per acre, to two millions yearly.

It is by the sale of those lands that the debt may be sunk, without burthen to any, and the quit-rent reserved thereon, will always lessen, and in time, will wholly support the yearly expence of government. It matters not how long the debt is in paying, so that the lands when sold be applied to the discharge of it, and for the execution of which, the Congress for the time being, will be the continental trustees.

I proceed now to the second head, viz. Which is the easiest and most practicable plan, RECONCILIATION or INDEPENDANCE; with some occasional remarks.

He who takes nature for his guide is not easily beaten out of his argument, and on that ground, I answer *generally—That* INDEPENDANCE *being a* SINGLE SIMPLE LINE, *contained within ourselves; and reconciliation, a matter exceedingly perplexed and complicated, and in which, a treacherous capricious court is to interfere, gives the answer without a doubt.*

The present state of America is truly alarming to every man who is capable of reflexion. Without law, without government, without any other mode of power than what is founded on, and granted by courtesy. Held together by an unexampled concurrence of sentiment, which, is nevertheless subject to change, and which every secret enemy is endeavouring to dissolve. Our present condition, is, Legislation without law; wisdom without a plan; constitution without a name; and, what is strangely astonishing, perfect Independance contending for dependance. The instance is without a precedent; the case never existed before; and who can tell what may be the event? The property of no man is secure in the present unbraced system of things. The mind of the multitude is left at random, and seeing no fixed object before them, they pursue such as fancy or opinion starts. Nothing is criminal; there is no such thing as treason; wherefore, every one thinks himself at liberty to act as he pleases. The Tories dared not have assembled offensively, had they known that their lives, by that act, were forfeited to the laws of the state. A line of distinction should be drawn, between, English soldiers taken in battle, and inhabitants of America taken in arms. The first are prisoners, but the latter traitors. The one forfeits his liberty, the other his head.

Notwithstanding our wisdom, there is a visible feebleness in some of our proceedings which gives encouragement to dissensions. The Continental Belt is too loosely buckled. And if something is not done in time, it will be too late to do any thing, and we shall fall into a state, in which, neither *Reconciliation* nor *Independance* will be practicable. The king and his worthless adherents are got at their old game of dividing the Continent, and there are not wanting among us, Printers, who will be busy in spreading specious falsehoods. The artful and hypocritical letter which appeared a few months ago in two of the New-York papers, and likewise in two others, is an evidence that there are men who want either judgment or honesty.

It is easy getting into holes and corners and talking of reconciliation: But do such men seriously consider, how difficult the task is, and how dangerous it may prove, should the Continent divide thereon. Do they take within their view, all the various orders of men whose situation and circumstances, as well as their own, are to be considered therein. Do they put themselves in the place of the sufferer whose *all* is *already* gone, and of the soldier, who hath quitted *all* for the defence of his country. If their ill judged moderation be suited to their own private situations *only*, regardless of others, the event will convince them, that "they are reckoning without their Host."

Put us, say some, on the footing we were on in sixty-three: To which I answer, the request is not *now* in the power of Britain to comply with, neither will she propose it; but if it were, and even should be granted, I ask, as a reasonable question, By what means is such a corrupt and faithless court to be kept to its engagements? Another parliament, nay, even the present, may hereafter repeal the obligation, on the pretence, of its being violently obtained, or unwisely granted; and in that case, Where is our redress?—No going to law with nations; cannon are the barristers of Crowns; and the sword, not of justice, but of war, decides the suit. To be on the footing of sixty-three, it is not sufficient, that the laws only be put on the same state, but, that our circumstances, likewise, be put on the same state; Our burnt and destroyed towns repaired or built up, our private losses made good, our public debts (contracted for defence) discharged; otherwise, we shall be millions worse than we were at that enviable period. Such a request, had it been complied with a year ago, would have won the heart and soul of the Continent—but now it is too late, "The Rubicon is passed."

Besides, the taking up arms, merely to enforce the repeal of a pecuniary law, seems as unwarrantable by the divine law, and as repugnant to human feelings, as the taking up arms to enforce obedience thereto. The object, on either side, doth not justify the means; for the lives of men are too valuable to be cast away on such trifles. It is the violence which is done and threatened to our persons; the destruction of our property by an armed force; the invasion of our country by fire and sword, which conscientiously qualifies the use of arms: And the instant, in which such a mode of defence became necessary, all subjection to Britain ought to have ceased; and the independancy of America, should have been considered, as dating its æra from, and published by, *the first musket that was fired against her*. This line is a line of consistency; neither drawn by caprice, nor extended by ambition; but produced by a chain of events, of which the colonies were not the authors.

I shall conclude these remarks, with the following timely and well intended hints. We ought to reflect, that there are three different ways, by which an independancy may hereafter be effected; and that *one* of those *three*, will one day or other, be the fate of America, viz. By the legal voice of the people in Congress; by a military power; or by a mob: It may not always happen that our soldiers are citizens, and the multitude a body of reasonable men; virtue, as I have already remarked, is not hereditary, neither is it perpetual. Should an independancy be brought about by the first of those means, we have every opportunity and every encouragement before us, to form the noblest purest constitution on the face of the earth. We have it in our power to begin the world over again. A situation, similar to the present, hath not happened since the days of Noah until now. The birthday of a new world is at hand, and a race of men, perhaps as numerous as all Europe contains, are to receive their portion of freedom from the event of a few months. The Reflexion is awful—and in this point of view, How trifling, how ridiculous, do the little, paltry cavellings, of a few weak or interested men appear, when weighed against the business of a world.

Should we neglect the present favorable and inviting period, and an Independance be hereafter effected by any other means, we must charge the consequence to ourselves, or to those rather, whose narrow and prejudiced souls, are habitually opposing the measure, without either inquiring or reflecting. There are reasons to be given in support of Independance, which men should rather privately think of, than be publicly told of. We ought not now to be debating whether we shall be independant or not, but, anxious to accomplish it on a firm, secure, and honorable basis, and uneasy rather that it is not yet began upon. Every day convinces us of its necessity. Even the Tories (if such beings yet remain among us) should, of all men, be the most solicitous to promote it; for, as the appointment of committees at first, protected them from popular rage, so, a wise and well established form of government, will be the only certain means of continuing it securely to them. *Wherefore*, if they have not virtue enough to be WHIGS, they ought to have prudence enough to wish for Independance.

In short, Independance is the only BOND that can tye and keep us together. We shall then see our object, and our ears will be legally shut against the schemes of an intriguing, as well, as a cruel enemy. We shall then too, be on a proper footing, to treat with Britain; for there is reason to conclude, that the pride of that court, will be less hurt by treating with the American states for terms of peace, than with those, whom she denominates, "rebellious subjects," for terms of accommodation. It is our delaying it that encourages her to hope for conquest, and our backwardness tends only to prolong the war. As we have, without any good effect therefrom, withheld our trade to obtain a redress of our grievances, let us *now* try the alternative, by *independantly* redressing them ourselves, and then offering to open the trade. The mercantile and reasonable part in England, will be still with us; because, peace *with* trade, is preferable to war *without* it. And if this offer be not accepted, other courts may be applied to.

On these grounds I rest the matter. And as no offer hath yet been made to refute the doctrine contained in the former editions of this pamphlet, it is a negative proof, that either the doctrine cannot be refuted, or, that the party in favour of it are too numerous to be opposed. WHEREFORE, instead of gazing at each other with suspicious or doubtful curiosity; let each of us, hold out to his neighbour the hearty hand of friendship, and unite in drawing a line, which, like an act of oblivion shall bury in forgetfulness every former dissension. Let the names of Whig and Tory be extinct; and let none other be heard among us, than those of *a good citizen, an open and resolute friend, and a virtuous supporter of the* RIGHTS *of* MANKIND *and of the* FREE AND INDEPENDANT STATES OF AMERICA.

To the Representatives of the Religious Society of the People called Quakers, or to so many of them as were concerned in publishing the late piece, entitled "THE ANCIENT TESTIMONY AND PRINCIPLES of the People called QUAKERS renewed, with Respect to the KING and GOVERNMENT, and touching the COMMOTIONS now prevailing in these and other parts of AMERICA addressed to the PEOPLE IN GENERAL."

The Writer of this, is one of those few, who never dishonours religion either by ridiculing, or cavilling at any denomination whatsoever. To God, and not to man, are all men accountable on the score of religion. Wherefore, this epistle is not so properly addressed to you as a religious, but as a political body, dabbling in matters, which the professed Quietude of your Principles instruct you not to meddle with.

As you have, without a proper authority for so doing, put yourselves in the place of the whole body of the Quakers, so, the writer of this, in order to be on an equal rank with yourselves, is under the necessity, of putting himself in the place of all those, who, approve the very writings and principles, against which your testimony is directed: And he hath chosen this singular situation, in order, that you might discover in him that presumption of character which you cannot see in yourselves. For neither he nor you can have any claim or title to *Political Representation.*

When men have departed from the right way, it is no wonder that they stumble and fall. And it is evident from the manner in which ye have managed your testimony, that politics, (as a religious body of men) is not your proper Walk; for however well adapted it might appear to you, it is, nevertheless, a jumble of good and bad put unwisely together, and the conclusion drawn therefrom, both unnatural and unjust.

The two first pages, (and the whole doth not make four) we give you credit for, and expect the same civility from you, because the love and desire of peace is not confined to Quakerism, it is the natural, as well the religious wish of all denominations of men. And on this ground, as men labouring to establish an Independant Constitution of our own, do we exceed all others in our hope, end, and aim. *Our plan is peace for ever.* We are tired of contention with Britain, and can see no real end to it but in a final separation. We act consistently, because for the sake of introducing an endless and uninterrupted peace, do we bear the evils and burthens of the present day. We are endeavoring, and will steadily continue to endeavour, to separate and dissolve a connexion which hath already filled our land with blood; and which, while the name of it remains, will be the fatal cause of future mischiefs to both countries.

We fight neither for revenge nor conquest; neither from pride nor passion; we are not insulting the world with our fleets and armies, nor ravaging the globe for plunder. Beneath the shade of our own vines are we attacked; in our own houses, and on our own lands, is the violence committed against us. We view our enemies in the character of Highwaymen and Housebreakers, and having no defence for ourselves in the civil law, are obliged to punish them by the military one, and apply the sword, in the very case, where you have before now, applied the halter—Perhaps we feel for the ruined and insulted sufferers in all and every part of the continent, with a degree of tenderness which hath not yet made its way into some of your bosoms. But be ye sure that ye mistake not the cause and ground of your Testimony. Call not coldness of soul, religion; nor put the *Bigot* in the place of the *Christian.*

O ye partial ministers of your own acknowledged principles. If the bearing arms be sinful, the first going to war must be more so, by all the difference between wilful attack and unavoidable defence. Wherefore, if ye really preach from conscience, and mean not to make a political hobby-horse of your religion, convince the world thereof, by proclaiming your doctrine to our enemies, *for they likewise bear* ARMS. Give us proof of your sincerity by publishing it at St. James's, to the commanders in chief at Boston, to the Admirals and Captains who are piratically ravaging our coasts, and to all the murdering miscreants who are acting in authority under HIM whom ye profess to serve. Had ye the honest soul of *Barclay* [1] ye would preach repentance to *your* king; Ye would tell the Royal Wretch his sins, and warn him of eternal ruin. Ye would not spend your partial invectives against the injured and the insulted only, but, like faithful ministers, would cry aloud and *spare none.* Say not that ye are persecuted, neither endeavour to make us the authors of that reproach, which, ye are bringing upon yourselves; for we testify unto all men, that we do not complain against you because ye are *Quakers*, but because ye pretend to *be* and are NOT Quakers.

> [1]"Thou hast tasted of prosperity and adversity; thou knowest what it is to be banished thy native country, to be over-ruled as well as to rule, and set upon the throne; and being *oppressed* thou hast reason to know how *hateful* the *oppressor* is both to God and man: If after all these warnings and advertisements, thou dost not turn unto the Lord with all thy heart, but forget him who remembered thee in thy distress, and give up thyself to follow lust and vanity, surely great will be thy condemnation.—Against which snare, as well as the temptation of those who may or do feed thee, and prompt thee to evil, the most excellent and prevalent remedy will be, to apply thyself to that light of Christ which shineth in thy conscience, and which neither can, nor will flatter thee, nor suffer thee to be at ease in thy sins."
>
> —*Barclay's address to Charles II.*

Alas! it seems by the particular tendency of some part of your testimony, and other parts of your conduct, as if, all sin was reduced to, and comprehended in, *the act of bearing arms*, and that by the *people* only. Ye appear to us, to have mistaken party for conscience; because, the general tenor of your actions wants uniformity: And it is exceedingly difficult to us to give credit to many of your pretended scruples; because, we see them made by the same men, who, in the very instant that they are exclaiming against the mammon of this world, are nevertheless, hunting after it with a step as steady as Time, and an appetite as keen as Death.

The quotation which ye have made from Proverbs, in the third page of your testimony, that, "when a man's ways please the Lord, he maketh even his enemies to be at peace with him";

is very unwisely chosen on your part; because, it amounts to a proof, that the king's ways (whom ye are desirous of supporting) do *not* please the Lord, otherwise, his reign would be in peace.

I now proceed to the latter part of your testimony, and that, for which all the foregoing seems only an introduction, viz.

"It hath ever been our judgment and principle, since we were called to profess the light of Christ Jesus, manifested in our consciences unto this day, that the setting up and putting down kings and governments, is God's peculiar prerogative; for causes best known to himself: And that it is not our business to have any hand or contrivance therein; nor to be busy bodies above our station, much less to plot and contrive the ruin, or overturn of any of them, but to pray for the king, and safety of our nation, and good of all men: That we may live a peaceable and quiet life, in all godliness and honesty; *under the government which God is pleased to set over us.*"—If these are *really* your principles why do ye not abide by them? Why do ye not leave that, which ye call God's Work, to be managed by himself? These very principles instruct you to wait with patience and humility, for the event of all public measures, and to receive *that event* as the divine will towards you. *Wherefore*, what occasion is there for your *political testimony* if you fully believe what it contains: And the very publishing it proves, that either, ye do not believe what ye profess, or have not virtue enough to practise what ye believe.

The principles of Quakerism have a direct tendency to make a man the quiet and inoffensive subject of any, and every government *which is set over him.* And if the setting up and putting down of kings and governments is God's peculiar prerogative, he most certainly will not be robbed thereof by us; wherefore, the principle itself leads you to approve of every thing, which ever happened, or may happen to kings as being his work. OLIVER CROMWELL thanks you. CHARLES, then, died not by the hands of man; and should the present Proud Imitator of him, come to the same untimely end, the writers and publishers of the Testimony, are bound, by the doctrine it contains, to applaud the fact. Kings are not taken away by miracles, neither are changes in governments brought about by any other means than such as are common and human; and such as we are now using. Even the dispersion of the Jews, though foretold by our Saviour, was effected by arms. Wherefore, as ye refuse to be the means on one side, ye ought not to be meddlers on the other; but to wait the issue in silence; and unless ye can produce divine authority, to prove, that the Almighty who hath created and placed this *new* world, at the greatest distance it could possibly stand, east and west, from every part of the old, doth, nevertheless, disapprove of its being independant of the corrupt and abandoned court of Britain, unless I say, ye can shew this, how can ye on the ground of your principles, justify the exciting and stirring up the people "firmly to unite in the *abhorrence* of all such *writings*, and *measures*, as evidence a desire and design to break off the *happy* connexion we have hitherto enjoyed, with the kingdom of Great-Britain, and our just and necessary subordination to the king, and those who are lawfully placed in authority under him." What a slap of the face is here! the men, who in the very paragraph before, have quietly and passively resigned up the ordering, altering, and disposal of kings and governments, into the hands of God, are now, recalling their principles, and putting in for a share of the business. Is it possible, that the conclusion, which is here justly quoted, can any ways follow from the doctrine laid down? The inconsistency is too glaring not to be seen; the absurdity too great not to be laughed at; and such as could only have been made by those, whose understandings were darkened by the narrow and crabby spirit of a despairing political party; for ye are not to be considered as the whole body of the Quakers but only as a factional and fractional part thereof.

Here ends the examination of your testimony; (which I call upon no man to abhor, as ye have done, but only to read and judge of fairly;) to which I subjoin the following remark; "That the setting up and putting down of kings," most certainly mean, the making him a king, who is yet not so, and the making him no king who is already one. And pray what hath this to do in the present case? We neither mean to *set up* nor to *put down*, neither to *make* nor to *unmake*, but to have nothing to *do* with them. Wherefore, your testimony in whatever light it is viewed serves only to dishonor your judgement, and for many other reasons had better have been let alone than published.

First, Because it tends to the decrease and reproach of all religion whatever, and is of the utmost danger to society, to make it a party in political disputes.

Secondly, Because it exhibits a body of men, numbers of whom disavow the publishing political testimonies, as being concerned therein and approvers thereof.

Thirdly, Because it hath a tendency to undo that continental harmony and friendship which yourselves by your late liberal and charitable donations hath lent a hand to establish; and the preservation of which, is of the utmost consequence to us all.

And here without anger or resentment I bid you farewell. Sincerely wishing, that as men and Christians, ye may always fully and uninterruptedly enjoy every civil and religious right; and be, in your turn, the means of securing it to others; but that the example which ye have unwisely set, of mingling religion with politics, *may be disavowed and reprobated by every inhabitant of* AMERICA.

F I N I S.

On Common Sense

"No writer has exceeded Paine in ease and familiarity of style, in perspicuity of expression, happiness of elucidation, and in simple and unassuming language."

Thomas Jefferson

"A pamphlet called 'Commonsense' makes a great noise. One of the vilest things that ever was published to the world. Full of false representations, lies, calumny, and treason, whose principles are to subvert all Kingly Governments and erect an Independent Republic."

Nicholas Cresswell

"I dreaded the effect so popular a pamphlet might have among the people, and determined to do all in my Power to counteract the effect of it."

John Adams

"Its effects were sudden and extensive upon the American mind. It was read by public men."

Dr. Benjamin Rush

"Have you read the pamphlet *Common Sense*? I never saw such a masterful performance.... In short, I own myself convinced, by the arguments, of the necessity of separation."

General Charles Lee

PREPARED FOR PUBLICATION BY
HISTORIC PUBLISHING

San Antonio, Texas

Made in the USA
Monee, IL
04 November 2026

67383327R10085